D0387617

ITALY

An Illustrated History

ITALY

An Illustrated History

DR. JOSEPH F. PRIVITERA

HIPPOCRENE BOOKS, INC.
New York

Copyright© 2000 Joseph F. Privitera

ISBN 0-7818-0819-7

For information, address:
HIPPOCRENE BOOKS, INC.
171 Madison Avenue
New York, NY 10016

Cataloging-in-Publication Data available from the Library of Congress

Printed in the United States of America.

DEDICATION

I dedicate this history

To my forefathers,

Whose bones lie buried

In Italian soil,

And to their American descendants:

My sister Angelina

And my sons,

Joe and Steve.

ACKNOWLEDGMENT

I am indebted to Kara Migliorelli, my gifted editor, who helped to produce a well-knit, readable text.

CONTENTS

Dedication v

Acknowledgment vi

Italy: The Cradle of Civilization xi

Preface xiii

Map xiv

The Boot, *Lo Stivale* 1
    476 A.D.: Enter the Barbarians and the Middle Ages 2
    The Lombards 6
    The Papacy 8
    The Frankish Emperors 8
    The Saracens 10
    The Normans 11
    The City-States 12
    Frederick II (1194–1250) 14

Italian: The Glue that Binds 14
    Dante Alighieri (1265–1321) 17

The Renaissance 21
    Cosimo de' Medici (1389–1464) 23
    Lorenzo the Magnificent (1449–1492) 25

The Other Powers   30
   The Kingdom of the Two Sicilies   30
   The Papal States   32
   Venice   40
   Genoa   41
   Milan   41
The High Renaissance   43

The Age of Invasions: 1495–1814   60
Charles VIII, King of France, Invades Italy   60
Louis XII, King of France, Follows Suit   61
Pope Julius II   63
Spanish-Austrian Ascendancy   64
Reign of Philip II   65
Extinction of the Old Ducal Families   67
The Decline of Venice and Spain   67
The Wars of Succession   68
Forty-Four Years of Peace   69

Italy in the Napoleonic Period: 1796–1814   70
Bonaparte in Italy   72

Il Risorgimento: 1815–1870   75
Austrian Rule in Italy   75
Reaction in the Italian States   76
The Carbonari   78
Revolutions of 1830   78
Mazzini, Garibaldi, and Cavour   79
   Giuseppe Mazzini (1805–1872)   80
   Giuseppe Garibaldi (1807–1882)   84

1860	88
1861	90
1862–1882	90
Count Camillo Benso di Cavour (1810–1861)	92
There was Prose, Poetry, and Music, Too	100
Giacomo Leopardi (1798–1837)	100
Alessandro Manzoni (1785–1873)	100
Giuseppe Verdi (1813–1901)	101
Forging A Modern Italy: 1871–1920	103
The Triple Alliance	105
Francesco Crispi (1818–1901)	105
Giovanni Giolitti (1842–1928)	106
End of the Triple Alliance	107
Italy Moves Toward War	107
Italy at War: 1915–1918	108
The Dark Age of Fascism: 1920–1945	109
Benito Mussolini (1883–1945)	109
The March on Rome, Via Sleeping Car	115
Il Duce: 1922–1939	116
1939 to 1945: The End	120
Reconstruction and Italy Today: 1945–2000	122
The Italian Republic	122
1948–1960	123
De Gasperi and the Christian Democrats	123
The Other Parties	125
The Economy Surges in the 1960s	125
Aldo Moro	126

The 1970s: Cultural Revolution and Terrorism   126
At the Threshold of the Twenty-First Century   128
The Cultural Scene   129

Afterword   139

Index   141

ITALY: THE CRADLE OF CIVILIZATION

A history shorn of a country's cultural element is not a true history of its people. An Italian history that does not also reflect the societal contributions of its poets, artists and musicians is untrue. Without Dante, Petrarch, Michelangelo, Vivaldi, Monteverdi, Ariosto, Alfieri, Verdi, Puccini, Manzoni, Quasimodo, and Pirandello, Italy's history is incomplete.

This history is written in the Renaissance mode, covering the full variety of Italy's achievements. We offer not a catalog, but a flavorful sampling of Italy's cultural contributions to the modern world.

PREFACE

Visit Rome, and the Roman Empire opens up before your eyes. Go to Florence, and the Renaissance and its art treasures leap up at you. Experience Sicily and its amalgam of cultures: the Phoenicians, the Ancient Greeks, the Romans, the Saracens, the Normans, and the Spaniards. Then add Italian, the beautiful tongue that binds it all together, plus one thousand hidden dialects, and you have Italy.

Map of Italy.

THE BOOT, *LO STIVALE*

Lo Stivale *(loh-stee-VAH-leh)* is what the Italians call their peninsula. A glance at the map indicates that Italy does indeed look like a boot. Flanked at the northwestern tip by the Alps and by its two islands, Sicily and Sardinia, at the southwestern tip, Italy is surrounded on all three sides by the waters of the Mediterranean.

An ethnically diverse population of over 58,000,000 live on Italy's 116,334 square miles. Neighbors to the north are France and Switzerland, and to the east, Austria and Slovenia.

The alluvial Po Valley drains most of the north. The rest of the country is rugged and mountainous, except for intermittent coastal plains, like the Campania, south of Rome. The Appenine Mountains run down through the center of the peninsula. Italy's largest cities are its capital, Rome, with a population of 2.8 million, Milan with 1.4 million, Turin with 962,000, and Naples with 1.1 million.

Italy is a republic with a president at the head of state and a prime minister at the head of government. Administratively, it consists of twenty *regioni* (regions), each with some autonomy, divided into ninety-five provinces. Parliament writes its laws.

About one quarter of the size of Cuba, Sicily covers an area of 9,926 square miles, and has a population of some five million. This *regione* embraces the island of Pantelleria (32 square miles) and the Lipari group (44 square miles), and includes two active volcanoes: Vulcano, at 1,637 feet, and Stromboli, at 3,038 feet. From prehistoric times, Sicily has been invaded, plundered and settled by more peoples than any other part of Italy, including the Siculi, Sicani, Phoenicians, Greeks, Romans, Vandals, Byzantines,

Saracens, Normans, Aragonese, Catalans, French, and Spanish Bourbons. Mount Etna, an active volcano, is Sicily's tallest peak at 11,053 feet.

Sardinia, the other major island, is 9,301 square miles and has a population of 1,647,000. Mountainous, it lies in the Mediterranean, 115 miles west of Italy and 7½ miles south of Corsica. In 1720 it was added to the possessions of the dukes of Savoy in Piedmont and Savoy to form the kingdom of Sardinia. Giuseppe Garibaldi, the hero of Italy's Unification, is buried on the nearby isle of Caprera. Elba, where Napoleon Bonaparte lived in exile from 1814–1815, is 86 square miles and lies 6 miles west of Tuscany.

476 A.D.: Enter the Barbarians and the Middle Ages

Today we might think of a barbarian as an uncouth, uncultivated individual. Not quite so in Roman times. To the Romans, any foreigner was a barbarian — that is, anyone who possessed language and customs different from their own, lived outside the pale of the Roman Empire or its civilization, or belonged to one of the northern nations who overthrew the empire.

During the fifth century, the principal barbarian tribes/ kingdoms were the Celts, who inhabited Scotland, Ireland, Cornwall, and in England, the Saxons, the Angles and the Jutes. On the continent, there were the Frankish, Danes, Alemanni, Burgundians, Goths, Ostrogoths, Heruli, and Vandals. From Asia, there were the Huns.

In 475, in the last days of the Roman Empire, Romulus, a handsome, wealthy young man, was proclaimed Emperor of Rome. He was deposed the following year by a barbarian general. That year, 476 A.D., marks the end of the Roman Empire in Italy.

The state the barbarians destroyed was one which, at its apogee, had stretched from Britain to the frontiers of Persia, and from the Rhine and Danube to the Sahara. It was an awesome empire which, for the first time in history, had ruled over many races — Etruscans, Ligurians, Iberians, Celts, Gauls, Basques, Greeks, Egyptians, Syrians, Armenians, Jews, and many others. The Empire was bound together by military and administrative efficiency, Roman law, and by a system of multi-directional highways. The Romans had created the most powerful and advanced nation on earth, encompassing every land and people within reach of its legions. Latin was their language.

The city of Rome stood at the head of this vast complex of peoples and nations. A steady stream of the spoils of war, taxes, tribute and gifts flowed into the *Urbs*, the City, from east and west, from north and south, creating the most powerful and the wealthiest city in the world. These riches, however, contained the seeds of decline and ultimate destruction; for, in the latter days of the Empire, society was divided into two classes: the very rich and the very poor. The great middle class, the nation's umbilical strength, had disappeared. Trades and the arts had been abandoned to slaves and serfs and, by the beginning of the fifth century, half of the Roman population were slaves. An affluent society had been reduced to an impotent mass. The great Roman Empire was no more and its lands and peoples were there for the taking by others with nascent vigor and greed. Enter the Barbarians.

The Colisseum in Rome.

The Pincio in Rome.

Odoacer (*c.* 435–493), king of the Heruli, a Germanic tribe, was a mercenary in the Roman service when, in 476, he turned on his masters. His troops attacked and defeated the Roman general, Orestes, at Piacenza. Ravenna, then the Roman capital, fell to Odoacer and he deposed Romulus, the last Roman emperor of the west.

The Empire was then subdivided: the western empire was at Ravenna, under Emperor Romulus; and the eastern empire was at Constantinople, under Emperor Zeno, who considered himself heir to the western Roman Empire. Zeno reluctantly recognized Odoacer's *de facto* authority over Italy and granted him the title of patrician. The Roman administration of Italy continued to function under Odoacer's rule. But in 488, still unhappy with this arrangement, Zeno sent Theodoric the Great, King of the Ostrogoths, into Italy to expel Odoacer. Theodoric made himself master of Italy, ordering the assassinations of Odoacer, his son, and his chief officers.

Theodoric began a long and beneficent rule over Italy; but after his death in 526, Justinian I, the Byzantine emperor who ruled the eastern part of the Roman Empire, expelled the Ostrogoths and the old Roman Empire was united again. Byzantine rule in Italy would ultimately collapse as a result of the invasion of the Lombards, another Germanic tribe.

The Lombards

Lombard domination in Italy lasted for over two hundred years (568–774). The Lombards are said to have been the fiercest and rudest of the Teutonic clans. Under their king, Alboin, they were a nation in movement. Pavia offered stubborn resistance, but after a three-year seige, the city was taken, and Alboin made it the capital of his new kingdom.

Having penetrated the peninsula, the Lombards occupied the Po Valley and moved slowly downward through the center of the country. Numerous though they were, they did not have enough strength to occupy the whole peninsula. Venice remained firm as did Genoa, both strong city-states. Ravenna, the new capital of the Roman Empire, remained a Greek city under the emperor of the eastern part of the empire. Rome, now under the protection of the papacy, escaped their onslaught. The seacoast cities of the south and the islands of Sicily, Sardinia, and Corsica preserved their independence. Thus, the Lombards neither occupied the extremities nor subjugated the brain-center of the country. The strength of Alboin's kingdom was in the north, in its capital of Pavia. As his people pressed southward, they failed to seize control of the coasts.

What was worse for the future of these conquerors, the original impetus of the invasion was checked by the untimely murder of Alboin in 573. After this event, the semi-independent chiefs of the Lombard tribe, who borrowed the title "duke" from their Roman predecessors, were content with consolidating their power in the districts each had occupied: the duchies of Spoleto in the center, and of Benevento in the south. Italy was now broken up into districts, with three separate capitals emerging: Pavia, the seat of the new Lombard kingdom; Ravenna, the garrison city of the Byzantine emperor; and Rome, the rallying point of the old nation, where the papacy was already beginning to assume the role of national protectorate.

The Papacy

The cornerstone of papal power was laid by two men: Benedict of Nursia (480–544) founded Western monasticism and put it at the service of the papacy; Pope Gregory I the Great (540–604) had the wisdom to reap the fruits of Benedict's work.

Gregory I initiated the Lombards' conversion to Catholicism. He made Rome a counterpoise against the effete Byzantine Empire at Constantinople on the one hand, and against the pressure of the feudal Lombard kingdom on the other. This policy was continued by his successors in the following century. Gregory II threw off allegiance to Byzantium and established the autonomy of Rome. He used the Lombards in his struggle with the Greeks, and in turn called upon the Franks to check the Lombards.

Pippin, the Frank king, twice crossed the Alps and forced the Lombards to relinquish their acquisitions, including Ravenna (the seat of the western Roman Empire), Pentapolis, the coastal towns of Romagna, and some cities in the duchy of Spoleto. These he handed over to the pope in 726. The virtual outcome of the silent struggle, begun in 726 by the popes against Byzantium and the Lombards, was to cut away the Lombards' power.

The Frankish Emperors

The Franko-Papal alliance, which conferred a crown on Pippin and sovereign rights upon the papacy, exercised a powerful influence in medieval history. In 774 Charlemagne (Charles the Great) deposed his father-in-law, Desiderius, the last Lombard

Bronze statuette of Charlemagne, the First Holy Roman Emperor.

king, and was crowned emperor in St. Peter's by Pope Leo III. This was a declaration to the world that the Roman Empire in the west was still alive, and that the popes created the emperors.

Charlemagne never succeeded in establishing firm control over Italy. His domain stretched from the Alps to Terracina, but it did not include most of the south, which still recognized the Byzantine emperor, the cities of Gaeta and Naples, South Apulia, Calabria, and Sicily.

When Charlemagne died in 814, he was succeeded by his son Louis I, who divided the empire among his sons. They, in turn, fought each other for territory, and their battles continued until Otto the Great, the king of Germany, was crowned emperor in 962. This marked the beginning of what was later called the Holy Roman Empire.

The Saracens

While Charlemagne's grandsons were fighting each other for a larger share of the domain, the Saracens were busily trying to gain a foothold in the south. Having overrun Spain, raided France repeatedly, and encircled and contained Byzantium in the east, they now threatened to seize control of the heart of Christendom. As early as the last years of Charlemagne, they had descended upon and sacked a town only forty miles from Rome. In 827 they invaded Sicily, and by 837 they were masters of the whole island. The Byzantines retired to their possessions on the mainland, but they were still not beyond the reach of Saracen pirates who, from their Sicilian bases, raided the coast of Italy up to the Tiber River. In 846 a band of Saracen troops disembarked in the vicinity of Rome and, after pillaging the countryside, advanced to the gates of Rome and sacked St. Peter's and St. Paul's, both of which were located outside the walls.

All of the southern provinces and duchies were taken by the troops, and many became Saracen strongholds. For a while, it seemed that Italy must undergo the fate of Spain and become a Moslem emirate. By the tenth century Sicily was the principal stronghold — and this is where the Normans come into play.

The Normans

In the tenth century the southern provinces of Italy were divided among the Byzantines, whose capital was at Bari, Apulia, in the "heel" of the Italian peninsula. On the other side of the "boot," on the Mediterranean coast, there were three duchies — Naples, Gaeta, and Amalfi — which had been part of the Greek domain, *Magna Graecia.* Though they were now autonomous, they still preserved some connection with the Greek Empire. The rest of the area was divided among the Lombards of Benevento, Capua and Salerno. The principalities, duchies and provinces had one thing in common: they all were weak and therefore were an easy prey for any prince or marauder with a strong army. The Normans were favored with such princes in abundance.

The Normans came from the north and settled in France, in the duchy of Normandy. Having recently been converted to Christianity, they made pilgrimages to the Holy Land, a voyage which satisfied both their newly acquired religious devotion and their love of adventure. During one of these voyages through southern Italy, a few Normans helped a local prince repel a

11

Saracen attack. They fought with such fervor and success that the prince invited them and their compatriots to settle in the neighborhood. The invitation was readily accepted, and these first settlers were followed by bands of Norman adventurers who fought against the Saracens, Greeks or the princes and dukes of southern Italy, depending upon who was paying them at the time. The Normans were, in effect, mercenaries — but mercenaries who liked the land and the people and decided to take root.

In 1042, dissatisfied with their payment from the Greek emperor for a war against the Saracens, the Normans invaded the province of Apulia, easily subdued it, and divided it among twelve brothers. One of the twelve, Robert Guiscard (Robert "the Cunning") of the de Hauteville family, took the sovereignty of Apulia for himself and invaded the remaining Greek province of Calabria, thus putting an end to the long reign of Constantinople in southern Italy (1057). A Greek influence had existed there for so long and had become so deeply ingrained that today many towns in the region still speak a dialect based on medieval Greek.

In 1061 Robert sent his younger brother, Roger, to rout the Saracens from Sicily, which they had dominated for two hundred years. He accomplished this in 1072, when he and his brother marched triumphantly through Palermo, the island's capital. They were given legitimate title to their conquest of the south of Italy and Sicily by Pope Nicholas II.

The City-States

From about the year 1000 on, Italian cities above Rome began to grow rapidly in independence and importance. They became centers of political life, banking, and foreign trade. Some became wealthy and many, including Florence, Genoa, Milan, Pisa and Venice, grew into nearly independent city-states. Venice, as late as the sixteenth century, had an ambassador in France, Marino Sanudo, who sent shrewd observations back to the Doge regarding the political and cultural life of Paris. These fascinating reports were written in the Venetian dialect, which was quite different from the high-Tuscan spoken elsewhere in Italy. One might recall Shakespeare's *Othello* and Arrigo Boito's adapted libretto for Verdi's *Otello*. In both the play and the opera, Othello is a noble Moor, serving as a general in the Venetian army. These city-states consistently managed to resist the efforts of noblemen and emperors to control them. They were truly the first independent political entities in Italy.

During the 1300s and 1400s some of these city-states ranked among the most important powers of Europe. But they were weakened by political disagreements among their citizens. The most famous division was between the Guelphs and Ghibellines; the Guelphs supported supreme rule by the pope, while the Ghibellines favored the emperor. They often took sides and waged war against each other. This weakened the city-states and resulted in their capture by foreign invaders.

With the Normans in the south, Italy soon had three major divisions: the Norman kingdom, itself; the states allied with, or under the control of, the papacy across the middle; and the Lombard kingdoms and growing maritime powers of Genoa, Pisa and Venice in the north.

In the twelfth century a strong ruler, Frederick Barbarossa, came down from Germany to claim his right to be crowned Holy Roman Emperor. Frederick was opposed in Italy by an alliance between the papacy and a Lombard League of cities, against which he struggled under the banner of the Hohenstaufens, known to Italians as the Ghibellines. The anti-imperial alliance became known as the Guelphs, and the conflict was the beginning of a number of Guelph-Ghibelline wars between coalitions of states led by the pope (Guelphs) and by emperors (Ghibellines) — wars which would darken Italy well into the Renaissance. Frederick was defeated, but his son, Henry VI, managed to seize the Sicilian kingdom.

Frederick II (1194–1250)

Henry's son, Frederick II, was the most gifted of the Holy Roman emperors. To his castles in Apulia and Sicily, he brought scholars, poets, astrologers (early astronomers), troubadour poets and lawyers. Frederick also founded the University of Naples, where he trained jurists to bring about his greatest reform: the reinstatement of a legal code based on Roman law.

Frederick II was a man of great learning and, as a dedicated poet, he formed the first school of poetry, known as the Sicilian School. Here, the first glimmerings of Italian, a national language, were put into verse.

ITALIAN: THE GLUE THAT BINDS

A nation that is aborning needs a common language to bind together its many disparate elements, both ethnic and linguistic. The Italian language served this function.

Portrait of Sicilian King Frederick II.

When the Roman Empire came apart, Latin, its principal language, also broke down. Depending on the nature of the local language onto which it had been grafted, Latin developed into new tongues, which today are called the Romance languages — that is, the languages of the Romans. In the Middle Ages, in northern France, Old French was developed and identified as the *langue d'oeil* (the language that uses the lexicon *oeil* to say *yes*). Over the centuries, Old French developed into today's polished Modern French. In the south of France, where a different language from the north was spoken, Latin broke down into Provençal, the *langue d'oc* (the language which uses the word *hoc* to say *yes*).

And so it went from country to country: in Spain, Latin broke down into Spanish, in Portugal, into Portuguese. But no matter where, the mother tongue had been Latin, Vulgar Latin, the language spoken by the *vulgus,* the people.

In Italy, Latin broke down into some five hundred dialects, with the dialect of one town differing from that of its neighbor, depending on the degree of isolation. In Tuscany (specifically Florence, Lucca, and Siena) and neighboring provinces, the Tuscan dialect was spoken. All writing, however, was in Latin. But as Tuscany's economy developed and prospered, and its citizens achieved a higher degree of physical comfort and well being, a small number of intellectuals, writers and poets began to write in the nascent "vulgar" tongue, the language of the people. Yet in so doing, they forged a more polished version than the common parlance which, though based on Tuscan, became separate and developed into the first tracings of Italian. This was the language that would serve as a beacon for the new country.

Dante Alighieri (1265–1321)

The man who, more than any other, helped develop Italian as a literary medium was Dante Alighieri. Born into a poor family of the minor nobility, he met his immortal love, Beatrice Portinari, at a May Day feast when both were nine years old. Though he did not meet her again until they were both eighteen and she had already married, Dante idealized his passion for her to such an extent that it dominated all of his poetry in the *Vita Nuova* and the *Divina Commedia*. Dante devoted considerable effort and attention to justifying the use of Italian as an appropriate literary medium. In the *Convivio* and the *De Vulgari Eloquentia*, he defended the use of Italian as opposed to Latin, which was still the only written language. He set forth his argument in Latin, not in Italian. But, as it happened, his example was far more potent than his theory.

There had been a first burst of poetry in Sicily where, under the leadership of Emperor Frederick II, a group of poets known as the Sicilian School first wrote poetry in the vernacular. Their verse forms, which imitated the popular Provençal poetry of southern France, became the first poetry to be written in a Romance language.

In this Provençal style of poetry, the poet longs for his lady fair and woos her from afar. The early Sicilian School poets were used as models by the northern poets, among them Dante, who began writing poetry in what was termed *il dolce stil nuovo,* the "sweet new style." Two metrical forms were used by the early Italian poets, the *canzone* (song or ode), derived from the Provençal, and the sonnet, which was of purely Italian origin, based on a Sicilian popular song with alternating rhymes.

17

Dante and Beatrice.

Dante's *Vita Nuova* is written both in prose and in a total of thirty-one poems, all of which idealize Beatrice as a creature more divine than earthly. This poetic device was used by the Provençal poets, but Dante enlarged it, especially in his *Divina Commedia*, which is divided into the Inferno, the Purgatory, and Paradise. But the *Commedia* clothes more than Dante's love for Beatrice; it is a judgment and commentary on his contemporaries and political enemies. He disapproved of the popes because they had become venal and developed temporal power to the detriment of the spiritual. Dante was a deeply religious man, who felt that the Church should divorce itself from political activities and lead the world in the true spirit of Christ. He therefore supported the Ghibellines against the Guelphs, the pope's adherents; and, as a result, he suffered a humiliating exile to Arezzo, Bologna, Padua, and Ravenna. Homeless and increasingly bitter, moving from one city to another, he continued writing his long poem. In his concept, the Inferno was the suffering and despair of his exile; Purgatory was his cleansing by faith, study, and writing; and Paradise was his redemption of hope through divine revelation and his unselfish love for Beatrice. He poured all that life had taught him into his great poem, finishing it only three years before his death. To many, the *Divina Commedia* is the greatest poem ever written.

But Dante was not alone in forging an elegant, lyrical tongue. There were others, including two equally famous poets, Petrarch and Boccaccio. Their contemporary was Giotto (*c.* 1266–1337), the outstanding painter of the early Renaissance, whose figures are graceful, dignified, natural, and individual.

Francesco Petrarca.

THE RENAISSANCE

Most of what had been characteristic of the Middle Ages had begun to decay by the fourteenth century. The Holy Roman Empire had collapsed; the universally recognized authority of the papacy had lost its prestige, and the dominant religious or spiritual interpretation of every phase of human life was undermined. Scholastic philosophy, which had been the inflexible guide of every intellect in Europe, had fallen into disrepute. In commerce, the ancient and tightly knit system of guilds in trade and industry had given way to the spirit of individual, free enterprise. There gradually appeared new institutions and new ways of thinking and living. The age during which this new civilization flourished in Italy, roughly from the beginning of the fifteenth century to the end of the sixteenth, is traditionally known as the Italian Renaissance.

To begin with, there was a revival of pagan learning. Virgil, Cicero, and Seneca were regarded as great authorities on almost every subject. No one excited more admiration than Aristotle, whose work was studied, analyzed, and memorized. In France, his writings on the theater led to the rule of the three unities — time, place and action — which governed the writing of drama.

But the Renaissance was much more than the revival of classical learning; it covered a multitude of new achievements in art, literature, philosophy, politics, education, science, and religion, some of which had little or nothing to do with the Greeks and Romans. It introduced a new complex of concepts, ideas, and ideals, which have set the standard for the modern world. Of these, perhaps the most important was that of humanism, which exalts the human and natural in life, rather than the divine and

Giotto's The Annunciation to St. Anne.

supernatural. Humanism included all of the ideals the Renaissance found worthy of pursuit: optimism, individualism, hedonism, skepticism, and materialism. The emphasis on this world, and on human values, was at the heart of the Renaissance.

Italy is where the Renaissance was born and flourished, and where the classical tradition was preserved more than anywhere else; Italians regarded themselves as the natural heirs of the ancient Romans and prided themselves on this heritage. Moreover, there was in Italy little of the dread which the Church inspired north of the Alps. The great universities, for example, were founded for the study of such subjects as law and medicine rather than, as elsewhere, of theology and scholastic philosophy. It was Italy which maintained the closest contact with the Byzantine and Saracenic civilizations and which absorbed the impact of their cultural influence. And it was in Italy where the cities flourished from commerce with the East, and where the accumulation of wealth provided leisure and the means for intellectual and artistic interests.

In Florence, the first glimmerings of the Renaissance appeared in the works of Dante, Petrarch, and Boccaccio. Just as it had its beginnings in Florence, the Renaissance invigorated the city once more in the first half of the fifteenth century. It was a movement that engaged not only artists but citizens as well. The epitome and paradigm of these citizens, and the most important figure of the early Renaissance, was Cosimo de' Medici.

Cosimo de' Medici (1389–1464)

A man without pretensions to artistic accomplishments, Cosimo de' Medici was the patron and friend of every artist of distinction.

Benvenuto Cellini's Bust of Cosimo I.

Largely due to Cosimo, the intellectual and artistic movement of the early fifteenth century flourished and gained momentum, bursting out of Italy and spilling into the rest of Europe.

These men of genius were principally Brunelleschi (1377–1446), Donatello (1386–1466), and Lorenzo Ghiberti (1378?–1455). The latter was a native of Florence who cast the bronze doors of the city's Baptistery — a door whose twenty right panels required twenty-one years to complete. This massive project required the aid of Donatello, Michelozzo, Brunelleschi, and a host of assistants.

The most famous painter of the period was a humble Dominican friar, a Tuscan named Guido di Pietro (1387–1455). He took the religious name of Fra Giovanni but came to be known as Fra Angelico, the "angelic brother." He was a patient, humble man, whose life was devoted to religion and painting, his personal form of prayer.

The antithesis of Fra Angelico was Fra Lippo Lippi (1406–1459), a man so susceptible to feminine beauty that he could not help painting Madonnas. His finest works are his depictions of the Virgin, who appears not as the idealized woman of Fra Angelico's paintings, but as a figure of sensuous beauty and warmth.

The humanists, encouraged and funded by Cosimo, were dedicated to the discovery, restoration and editorial revision of the Greek and Latin classics. Plato, Virgil, Cicero, and Horace were the heroes of the humanists.

Lorenzo the Magnificent (1449–1492)

Piero de' Medici, who succeeded his father, Cosimo, was not the elder's equal in intelligence and tact. During his tenure, the city was in revolt. Piero was succeeded by Lorenzo, who became known as "the Magnificent." Like his grandfather, he stood at the center of a brilliant group of scholars, artists, sculptors, and poets. Under Lorenzo, the Renaissance spread to Lombardy and Calabria. All other cities strove to imitate Florence.

Lorenzo was the embodiment of the ideal Renaissance prince — a modest, dignified, and adept statesman. After statecraft, his chief interest was the pursuit of knowledge. His morals reflected those of the humanists of the time. He wrote devout hymns and licentious verses with equal facility and enthusiasm. Taking great care to maintain the outward appearance of religious devotion, he erstwhile amused himself with a steady stream of mistresses, many of whom turned out to be the wives of prominent Florentines. He supported religious causes and, with equal generosity, a host of virtually pagan artists, writers, poets, sculptors, and scholars.

Just as his grandfather, Cosimo, had been in the Early Renaissance, Lorenzo was the most magnificent patron of the High Renaissance, ruling a powerful state and at the same time managing and increasing one of Europe's greatest fortunes.

Perhaps the most remarkable man of Lorenzo's circle was Pico della Mirandola (1463–1494), the paradigm of the universal genius of the Renaissance. He was interested in everything — philosophy, poetry, architecture, music — and he excelled at everything he studied.

Lorenzo's interests extended, like those of his grandfather, to architecture, sculpture, and painting, and he gave a pension to any student who showed talent or promise. One such prospect was Michelangelo Buonarroti.

The Lady of the Primroses, *thought to be Lucrezia Donati, mistress of Lorenzo the Magnificent. Sculpture of Verrocchio (1435–1488).*

During Lorenzo's reign, Florence became home to some of Europe's most elegant residences and public buildings. The Strozzi family of bankers had a splendid residence built in Florence, known as the Strozzi Palace.

The finest sculptor of the time was Andrea di Michele Cione, known to posterity as Verrocchio, a master of anatomy. His greatest work was his *David*; the Florentine Signory so admired this work that they placed it at the head of the main stairway of the Palazzo Vecchio.

Sculpture, however, was gradually being replaced by painting. One outstanding painter of the day was Sandro Botticelli (1447?–1510) who, after serving as apprentice to Fra Filippo Lippo, began to receive commissions from the Medicis. For Lucrezia Tournabuoni, Lorenzo's mother, Botticelli painted *Judith*; and for Lorenzo, he painted *The Birth of Venus* and *Primavera* (Spring). The latter is perhaps his best known painting today.

Such were some of the chief figures who comprised the circle of Lorenzo the Magnificent during the Golden Age of the Florentine Renaissance. It was in the midst of all this activity that Lorenzo died, on April 9, 1492, at the age of forty-three. On his deathbed, he expressed to Pico della Mirandola and to Poliziano his regret that he must die before completing the collection of manuscripts he had undertaken. "He lived long enough for his glory," said King Ferdinand of Naples, "but he lived too short a time for Italy."

Lorenzo was the most remarkable prince of the fifteenth century; but there were others who patronized scholars and artists. In almost every northern city, except in Piedmont, rulers and citizens alike were fond of art and had an artist of whom they were proud. But as long as Lorenzo lived, Florence was the most

Botticelli's The Birth of Venus.

outstanding of the cities of Italy, and the most envied. Upon his death, however, intellectual and artistic primacy was to pass from Florence to Rome.

The Other Powers

During the Renaissance, six principal states emerged in Italy — the Kingdom of the Two Sicilies, the Papal States, Venice, Genoa, Florence, and Milan — all varying greatly in character, but more or less equal in importance. Florence developed into the country's principal power and undisputed cultural leader, but other power centers also evolved during the Renaissance.

The Kingdom of the Two Sicilies

At the beginning of the fourteenth century, Robert of Anjou succeeded his father as Count of Anjou and Provence, and King of Sicily. As Count of Provence, where the popes were resident in his dominions of Avignon, Robert served as a link between the papacy and Italy. Although he had possessions in Piedmont, his court was in Naples where, under his rule, the University of Naples attracted students from all parts of Italy. Tuscan painters and sculptors found his capital a welcoming place of work. There was a sharp contrast, however, between the civilized life of the capital and the rest of the kingdom. Robert lived under a constant menace from the lower peninsula and Sicily, where the nobles reigned like petty sovereigns over their estates.

When Robert died in 1343, his frivolous granddaughter, Joanna, assumed the throne. In the thirty-eight years of her reign,

Italy in the 15ᵀᴴ and 16ᵀᴴ centuries.

Queen Joanna managed to reduce Naples to the same state of degradation as Sicily. Her kingdom was seized by a cousin, Charles of Durazzo, who ruled for four years (1382–1386). Charles was succeeded in turn by his son and daughter.

In Sicily, the Norman royal line was replaced by the Spanish House of Aragon (1409). While the House of Anjou still claimed Naples for itself, there followed a struggle between Frenchmen and Spaniards, which proved disastrous to the entire peninsula; it ended in 1443, when Alfonso of Aragon was recognized by the pope as King of the Two Sicilies. Thus, by the middle of the fifteenth century, the southern half of Italy was united and at peace.

Charles VIII crossed the Alps as an ally of Milan in 1492, while Florence, Naples, and the papacy combined their efforts to resist his invasion. Charles VIII made himself master of Naples almost unhindered. Yet he was back in France little more than a year after first crossing the Alps, so that by the end of 1496 his Italian conquest had melted away. Spanish troops were sent by Ferdinand the Catholic to re-establish the Aragonese in Naples. After an agreement between France and Spain, the Aragonese line was dispossessed and the kingdom of Naples was divided between the two powers. A few years later the French were ousted, and the entire ancient Sicilian kingdom was once more united under the rule of Spain.

The Papal States

During the absence of the popes from Italy (1305–1376), the cities belonging to the papacy set up despots, who paid nominal allegiance to the pope and ruled as independent princes. In the early years of the fourteenth century a power struggle ensued between the papacy and the Este family for control of Ferrara. By skilful diplomacy and by playing off the papacy against Venice, the Este brothers preserved the independence of Ferrara and were recognized by the pope as his vicars. Thanks to the Este family, Ferrara attained worldwide recognition as a center of civilization.

With the law school of its university famous throughout Europe, the city of Bologna had an importance beyond its size. In the first half of the fourteenth century, it enjoyed an interlude of peace under the lordship of the local house of Pepoli.

While no longer the pope's residence, Rome became one of the cities in the Papal States in which local powerful families, the Orsini and the Colonna, struggled for supremacy. It was Rienzi, half hero, half charlatan, who captured the imagination of the Romans and was proclaimed Tribune of the People in 1347. Rienzi's statements and actions indicated his intention to rule all of Italy under the aegis of the Roman Republic. But when both the pope and emperor were alarmed by his pretensions, he was forced to flee the city; within a year of his rise to power, an insurrection took place and Rienzi was put to death.

Pope Urban returned to Italy in 1367, but unable to establish his power in Rome he returned to Avignon in 1370. However, when Gregory VI returned to Rome in January 1377, he was able to remain; and when he died a year later, the Italian Urban VI was elected to succeed him, followed six months later by Clement VII, who returned to Avignon. The existence of rival popes seriously weakened the Roman pontiff's hold over his Italian dominions. It was not until Martin V returned to Rome in 1421 that the papacy was restored to its historical place in Rome, making the city a splendid Renaissance capital.

One of the most important developments of the fifteenth century was the emergence of the papacy as an Italianized temporal power. When the Council of Constance ended the Great Schism by electing Martin V as pope, the task confronting the papacy was the recovery of its lost prestige. Martin and his successors sought to regain this by creating an Italian state which could hold its own against its neighbors and identify the papacy with literary and artistic movements of the time. Martin V was a Colonna — a great advantage, as he could rely upon his family's support in the College of Cardinals and in the city of Rome. With their help, he gained some measure of recognition for his authority throughout the States of the Church. To the Romans, his reign brought a return of order and prosperity and the restoration of the city's half-ruined buildings.

Eugenius IV, Martin V's successor, had difficulties with the Council of Basel; his enemies fomented a revolution in Rome, setting up a republican government and forcing him to flee for his life. He spent several years of his exile in Florence, where he became acquainted with Greek scholars and the artistic and literary interests of the Florentines. When he was able to return to Rome, Eugenius gave Florentine humanists posts as papal secretaries and employed Florentine painters and sculptors at the Vatican.

Eugenius IV's successor, Nicholas V (1447–1455), was himself a professional humanist. Having studied at the University of Bologna, he won the notice of a cardinal who made him his secretary and set him on the path leading to the papal throne. In his early days, Nicholas V said that if he were ever rich, he would spend his money on books and buildings. As pope, he realized these ambitions to the fullest. He set scholars to translate Greek and employed agents to search Europe for manuscripts. The Vatican Library soon became a center for classical studies.

Among the popes of the fifteenth century, Pius II (1458–1464), like Nicholas V, was a humanist and perhaps the best speaker and man of letters ever to wear the papal tiara. The pontificate of Sixtus IV (1471–1484) is marked by his determination to turn the states of the Church into a strong, well-armed dominion. Under Innocent VIII (1484–1492), the secularization of the papacy continued. With the accession of Rodrigo Borgia as Alexander VI (1492–1503), the position of the papacy was that of a temporal Italian power. Rome was distinguished from other centers of the Renaissance by its greater extravagance and open vice.

Alexander VI was succeeded by the brief pontificate of Pius III and then by Cardinal Giuliano della Rovere, who in 1503 took the name of Julius II. Strengthening the Church was Julius' consistent aim, and he was determined to recover full possession of the states of the Church. With the exception of the states seized by the Este in Ferrara, Julius II was master throughout his dominions.

Under the pontifical hand of Julius, Rome came full-blown into the High Renaissance. Artists and men of letters, lacking employment throughout the fall of so many princely patrons, came to Rome in search of fresh opportunities. They found them in the pope's grandiose schemes for the enrichment of his capital.

With Bramante as chief architect, the foundation stone of the new St. Peter's was laid and the Vatican galleries were built. Raphael began work on his series of frescoes in the pope's private apartments; Michelangelo decorated the ceiling of the Sistine Chapel and prepared sculptures for the great tomb, which Julius

Pope Nicholas V, founder of the Vatican Library; he died in Rome in 1455.

Obyt Anecua · Anno 1564. ÆNEAS SYLVIVS

PICOLOMINEVS, dictus PIVS II

Pont. Max. Nat. Colmunj A° 1500.

Ut pius Æneas, ut et alter Sylvius esset,
Ductor & Oenotriæ Pastor in urbe fuit.

The Humanist Pope Pius II (1405–1464), protector of Rome's monuments.

37

Milozzo da Forlì's fresco of Pope Sixtus IV, the Creator of the Sistine Chapel.

The Borgia Pope, Alexander VI (1431–1503).

had ordered to serve as a memorial of his pontificate. In place of the medieval city, with its narrow, filthy streets and its fortress-like palaces, a new and spacious Rome of the Renaissance came into being.

Julius II's ambitions extended beyond Rome and the Papal States: he aimed to unite all of Italy under his leadership and free it of the foreigner. But he achieved only limited success; by the time he died, Italy had been freed from the French at the high price of increasing the power of the Swiss and the Spanish.

Venice

Trade with the East was in Venetian hands. Geographical location and an energetic citizenry combined to make Venice the focal point of medieval commerce. At the height of its power, Venice held Crete, Corfu, many islands in the Aegean, and the Dalmatian coast from Trieste to Albania. Treaty rights at Constantinople, Trebizond, Alexandria, and other ports made the Black Sea and the eastern Mediterranean free to its vessels.

Twice a year, beginning in the fourteenth century, a fleet of galleys set sail from Venice, taking with them spices, sugar, pepper, and other eastern products by way of Gibraltar and Southampton to Bruges. The fleet returned laden with Scandinavian wood and furs, English wool, Flemish cloth, and French wines. Other goods from the East were conveyed on pack-horses across the Alps to supply the needs of German cities. A treaty with the Turks in 1299 ensured Venice protection for pilgrimages to Palestine made under its auspices. The result was a monopoly of tourist traffic — pilgrims from all parts of Europe, sailing in the Venetian galleys to visit the Holy Places of Christendom.

Genoa

Among the Italian cities in the fourteenth century, Genoa was Venice's only maritime rival. At the naval battle of Meloria in 1282, Genoa inflicted a defeat on its neighbor and rival, Pisa. From that time on, Pisan power and prosperity began to decline, and in 1406 Pisa was conquered by Florence. Genoa's attempt to exercise control over Corsica and Sardinia was disputed by the Aragonese kings of Naples. Genoa maintained its supremacy and the administration of Corsica through its great trading corporation, the Bank of St. George. Sardinia, however, was finally conquered by the Aragonese. The coast of North Africa became a special sphere of Genoese commercial activity, where merchants established trading colonies and penetrated the interior in search of gold.

In the East, the rivalry between Venice and Genoa was unceasing. Genoa won more than one naval victory at the expense of Venice during the course of their struggle. The superior seamanship of the Genoese commanders won battles at Curzola (1298) and Sapienza (1354), and brought the war to the gateway of Venice in the war of Chioggia (1379–1380). However, the end of the fourteenth century saw the decline of Genoa as a naval power, leaving Venice the undisputed mistress of the seas. The acceptance of French suzerainty in 1396 marked both the end of the independent republic and the beginning of Genoa's decline as a commercial and colonial power.

Milan

Henry VII's granting of an Imperial Vicariate to Matteo Visconti during his Italian expedition marked the final victory of the

Visconti family over the rival house of della Torre. For the past sixty years, both families had vied for control of Milan. After Henry VII's death in 1313, Matteo gave protection to neighboring cities such as Pavia and Cremona, which were threatened by Robert of Naples, and received in return an acknowledgement of his supremacy. This was the beginning of the Visconti dominion, both east and west of Milan, which would continue throughout the century. During Gian Galeazzo Visconti's (1379–1402) career, the Visconti lordship rose above other despotisms of the Lombard plain. Gian extended his control over neighboring cities, collected taxes, and executed justice throughout his dominion. The cathedral of Milan was built under his orders. Gian's prestige grew so that the Visconti were accepted by the princely families of Europe. Gian's first wife was Isabella of France, the king's daughter. His sister married Lionel, Duke of Clarence, and his nieces married into the ruling houses of Austria and Bavaria.

From his duchy of Milan, Gian's conquering armies pressed forward until they seemed about to bring all of Italy under his control. In the north, his power extended from the frontiers of Piedmont to Padua. South of the River Po, he controlled the Via Emilia from Piacenza to Bologna and established a protectorate over Romagna. His possession of Lucca, Pisa, and Piombino cut off Florence from the sea, while his occupation of Siena and Perugia blocked the two main roads to Rome. In August 1402, when all hope seemed lost, Gian Galeazzo died of fever, and Florence was saved. To achieve his conquests, however, Gian had stretched his resources to the breaking point; thus, he left behind an exhausted dominion, which broke up into pieces when his strong hand was removed.

Soon after the death of Filippo Maria Visconti in 1447, Milan passed into the control of Francesco Sforza, the son of a soldier from Romagna. Francesco assumed his father's command, fighting first for Milan and then for Venice. He was so successful that Filippo Maria Visconti sought to attach him to the family by marrying him to Bianca, his illegitimate daughter. When Milan declared itself a republic, Francesco Sforza was forced to serve the republican government as its captain. But he had higher ambitions. After turning his forces against Milan, Sforza was able to starve the city into surrender and force the chief assembly of the republic to acclaim him as the successor of the Visconti (1450).

There followed a defensive league between Milan, Florence, and Venice, to which Alfonso of Naples gave his adherence, and which Pope Nicholas V ratified with his blessing. The Italian League of 1455 represents the nearest Italy came to unity in the fifteenth century. Designed to prevent any one of the greater powers from increasing at the expense of its weaker neighbors, it also stood for a common national front against external attack. The League secured a respite from serious warfare, which enabled the members of each city-state to concentrate their energies upon the arts of peace. The outcome was a significant contribution to civilization.

The High Renaissance

The first quarter of the sixteenth century, the *cinquecento*, is the period of the High Renaissance. The intellectual and artistic revolution that first began in Florence was now approaching its period of culmination — one in which the greatest masters were to do their work. This era produced the finest writers since Petrarch, the greatest architects since the Gothic masters of the Ile-de-France, the greatest sculptors since Praxiteles, and the greatest painters the world had ever seen.

Italian literature came alive brilliantly. Niccolò Machiavelli (1469–1527) was by far the most famous writer on statecraft, which was fully expressed in his celebrated work, *The Prince*. He was also author of the outstanding comedy of the Renaissance, *La Mandragola* (The Mandrake).

In poetry, *Orlando Furioso* (The Mad Roland) by Lodovico Ariosto (1474–1533) describes the heroic events of Italy's past. Kept alive in even the most remote areas of the country, these stories continue to be an integral part of Italian folklore.

Michelangelo is widely regarded as a great painter and sculptor. A man of universal genius, he was also a poet of the first rank who wrote sonnets and madrigals in the *Vita Nuova* tradition.

The *cinquecento* produced a score of famous men, among whom four stand out: Leonardo, Bramante, Raphael, and Michelangelo.

Leonardo da Vinci (1452–1519) was a Florentine, trained by Verrocchio. By the time he was twenty-five, he was already highly esteemed as a painter and had won the attention and favor of Lorenzo the Magnificent. After several years under Lorenzo's patronage, he accepted an offer of employment at the court of the Sforzas in Milano, where he spent sixteen years. A true Renaissance man, Leonardo did everything that excited his creative genius: he painted portraits, drew architectural designs, executed hydraulic works, studied the cultivation of the grape, and played his silver lyre. He painted one of his surviving masterpieces in the Dominican refectory of Santa Maria della Grazie: a fresco of the Last Supper, which is still being restored.

Leonardo's best-known work is perhaps the *Mona Lisa*, a portrait of the wife of Francesco del Giocondo, a Neapolitan. It is the most imitated painting in the history of art, for it portrays a universal likeness of woman — a woman with an enigmatic smile.

The greatest architect of the High Renaissance was Donato d'Agnolo, called Bramante of Urbino (1444–1514). Like Leonardo, he worked in Milan during the reign of Lodovico Sforza, but he achieved fame in Rome, where he became the papal architect of Innocent VIII and Julius II. He shares with Raphael and Michelangelo the honor of having shaped the Basilica of St. Peter and the Vatican palace.

Upon Bramante's death, the reigning pope, Leo X, appointed the painter Raffaello Sanzio as his successor. Better known as Raphael (1483–1520), he would find fame as history's most successful, beloved, and cheerful artist. He was born in Urbino, where his father, Giovanni de' Santi, was a court painter and poet of the duke. At the age of eleven, Raphael began studying painting under a local master. In 1500 he went to Perugia, where he studied under the celebrated Perugino.

Raphael then went to Florence, where he became a pupil of both Leonardo and Michelangelo, under whose tutelage his technique began to evolve. At that time, he painted a series of Madonnas, all of which reveal the influence of Leonardo. By 1508 his fame had already reached Rome, and Pope Julius invited him to come to the City. There, he created some of the noblest monuments of the High Renaissance: his frescoes in the Vatican palace. In his art, Raphael devoted himself to the cultivation of ideal beauty as an end in itself. And it is this quality that has endeared him to succeeding generations as well as to his own.

Leonardo da Vinci's
Mona Lisa.

Leonardo da Vinci's
Madonna Benois.

Raphael's Portrait of Agnolo Doni.

Raphael's The Veiled Lady.

Raphael's The Wedding of the Virgin.

Raphael's The Sistine Madonna.

Raphael's Galatea.

The towering figure of the High Renaissance was Michelangelo Buonarroti (1475–1564), born in the little town of Caprese, near Florence, where his family moved when he was six. At the age of thirteen, he was apprenticed to Ghirlandaio, the city's most popular and successful painter. Michelangelo's early work as a sculptor attracted the attention of Lorenzo, who took him into the Medici palace. Together with other artists and poets, he became a member of the prince's most intimate circle. Michelangelo remained at the palace until Lorenzo's death in 1492 and then went on to Bologna, returning to Florence in 1495. The following year, he went to Rome, where he obtained the patronage of Cardinal Raffaello Riario. There, he sculpted his masterpiece, the *Pietà*.

The success of his *Pietà* brought Michelangelo fame, money, and also an important commission from Florence, whose cathedral, for a century, had possessed an enormous, irregularly shaped raw block of marble. Michelangelo was asked to chisel a statue out of it. The result was a statue which the Florentines called *il gigante*, the giant, and which came to be known as *David.* In the opinion of Vasari: "It surpasses every other statue, ancient or modern, Latin or Greek."

In 1541, after six years of labor, Michelangelo completed what was perhaps his most famous painting, *The Last Judgment*, behind the altar of the Sistine Chapel in Rome. Artists came from all over Europe to study the anatomy and musculature of the figures, as well as the amazing sense of perspective.

Michelangelo continued working until his death at the age of eighty-nine. He was buried in Florence, where his great admirer, Vasari, declared him to be the greatest artist who ever lived.

Engraving after a self-portrait of Michelangelo.

Portrait of Giovanna Albizzi Tornabuoni, *by Domenico Ghirlandaio.*

Michelangelo's The Pietà.

Michelangelo's Head of David.

Michelangelo's The Prophet Jeremiah.

Michelangelo's Bust of Brutus.

Michelangelo's Piety and Majesty. *The statue has stood in a small church in Bruges, Belgium for 450 years.*

The *cinquecento* closed just as the Renaissance came to an end, and Italy entered into one of its most turbulent periods in history.

THE AGE OF INVASIONS: 1495–1814

The year 1492 is a memorable date in Italian history, one remembered as the year Columbus discovered America. The gradual destruction of Venice's commercial supremacy was one result of the discovery of the New World. It is also the year for the following: Lorenzo died and was succeeded by his son, the vain and weak Piero; France passed into the personal control of the inexperienced Charles VIII; the fall of Granada freed Spain from its embarrassments; and Roderigo Borgia assumed the tiara as Alexander VI. In 1492 the short-lived federation of the five powers was shaken, and Italy was once more drawn into the vortex of European affairs. What follows is the tale of neighbors, allies, and enemies making a grab for pieces of Italy. Greed, power, and riches were surely incentives for all of the participants. Looking back on this period, it is a wonder how Italy escaped from the foibles of both friends and enemies.

Charles VIII, King of France, Invades Italy

After the assassination of Galeazzo Maria Sforza of Milan in 1476, his crown passed to the young Gian Galeazzo, who later married a granddaughter of Ferdinand I of Naples. But the government of Milan remained in the hands of Gian's uncle,

Lodovico, surnamed *Il Moro* (The Moor), who was determined to become Duke of Milan.

The King of Naples was Lodovico's natural enemy, and the latter had cause to suspect that he would not receive support in his quest from Piero dei Medici. Feeling alone, and with no right to the title he was bent on seizing, Lodovico turned to Charles VIII of France, whom he urged to make good on his claim to the kingdom of Naples. After some hesitation, Charles agreed to invade Italy; he crossed the Alps in 1495, passed through Lombardy, entered Tuscany, freed Pisa from Florence's control, witnessed the expulsion of the Medici, marched to Naples and was crowned there — all this without striking a blow.

Meanwhile, Lodovico had his nephew assassinated and then formed a league to oust the French from Lombardy. Charles hurried back from Naples, barely escaping entrapment and death. He managed to return unscathed to France in 1495. While little remained of his easy acquisitions, he had managed to convulse Italy by his invasion, destroying its equilibrium and exposing its military weakness and political disunion. But worse still, he had revealed Italy's wealth to greedy and more powerful nations.

Louis XII, King of France, Follows Suit

The Spanish House of Aragon was not idle either; now represented by Frederick, it returned to Naples. Florence had become a republic and had adopted a constitution analogous to that of Venice. But the monk Girolamo Savonarola was actually in charge, and was feared by all for his fanaticism. Preaching religious reformation, he was a challenge to Rome and a thorn in its side. When he eventually lost his hold on the people who feared him, Pope Alexander VI set up a mock trial and condemned him to death. He was assassinated and burned at the stake in the Piazza in 1498.

That year, Louis XII succeeded Charles VIII to the French throne. As Duke of Orleans, Louis XII had certain claims to Milan through his grandmother, Valentina, who was the daughter of Gian Galeazzo, the first duke of Milan. Yet Louis XII's claims were not valid, for the duchy had been granted only to male heirs, which invalidated his claim through his grandmother.

However, all Louis XII needed was a pretext, and in 1499 he crossed the Alps and seized Milan. Lodovico escaped to Germany, but was betrayed by his Swiss mercenaries who shipped him to France to die at Loches. This disposed of the Sforzas in Milan.

The following year, Louis made the mistake of calling upon the Spanish king, Ferdinand the Catholic, to help him seize Naples. Both kings signed a treaty at Granada in which they agreed to divide the spoils. The conquest proved to be easy, but the thieves fell out over the spoils, with Ferdinand playing the Frenchman false when he placed the Two Sicilies under his Crown. Two years later, more skulduggery occurred; Louis XII signed another treaty, the Treaty of Blois (1504), whereby he invited the emperor Maximilian to help him subjugate Venice. No move could have been more foolhardy. In signing the treaty, Louis had helped to create the future major rival of France.

The stage was now set, and all of the actors who were to help bring about the ruin of Italy moved in with their armies. Spain, France, and Germany with its Swiss mercenaries, used various pretexts to divide Italy's provinces among themselves. During the next quarter of a century, these players were actively engaged in carving up the peninsula and its islands. There was no one to challenge them, not even the peninsula's petty rulers.

Pope Alexander VI was the only one who managed to make any gains. Aided by his son, Cesare Borgia, he chastised the Roman nobles, subdued Romagna and the March, threatened Tuscany, and seemed on the point of creating a unified Italy under Cesare, when he died suddenly in 1503.

Pope Julius II

Julius II, Alexander's most bitter enemy, succeeded him to the papal throne and continued his predecessor's policies, but no longer in the interest of his own relatives. His ambition was to aggrandize the Church and to reassume the protectorate of the Italian people. With this in mind, he obtained control of Emilia, subdued Ferrara, and cut back the tyranny of the Baglioni in Perugia. In 1508 he quarreled with the Venetians and combined the forces of all Europe against them. When Julius II had completely subdued them, he resolved, in 1510, to expel the foreigners from Italy by pitting the Spaniards against the French. He hoped to enlist the help of the Swiss, but this proved ineffective. The Battle of Ravenna was fought between the French and Julius II's allies — the Spaniards, Venetians, and Swiss — who managed to expel the French from Lombardy. But in the main, Julius II had failed.

In 1513 Julius II was succeeded by Leo X, and the same struggle resumed, more fiercely than ever. There was a quick succession of events, culminating in the sacking of Rome in 1527.

The city was abandoned to a marauding party of thirty thousand foreign ruffians.

Spanish-Austrian Ascendancy

Charles V, King of Castile and Aragon, entered the scene on November 5, 1529, when he was crowned emperor by Clement VII. At that time, Italy was divided as follows: Venice's freedom and its control of the Lombard territories were respected; the Este family remained in control of their duchy of Modena, Reggio, and Ferrara; and the Medici continued to rule Florence. The one to gain the most during this period was the pope, who held the most substantial Italian province. The rest of Italy, however, became a dependence of Spain. Charles V, now emperor, appointed Spanish viceroys in Milan and Naples. Moreover, he was supported by the pope and by the minor princes who slavishly followed the policy dictated to them from Madrid.

From 1530 until 1796, a period of nearly three centuries, the Italians had no history of their own. Their annals are filled with records of dynastic changes and redistributions of territory, resulting from treaties signed by foreign powers in the settlement of quarrels. Italy became the scene of wars fought by alien armies. The points at issue were decided beyond the Alps, with the gains accruing to royal families. The Italians were haggled over by the Hapsburgs and the Bourbons, like oxen driven to market by greedy farmers. It was a period during which Italy was defenseless and helpless, under the control of powerful foreign nations. That it had created modern civilization for Europe availed it not at all. Italy had entered an age of slavery.

In 1534 Alessandro Farnese, who owed his elevation to the papacy to his sister Giulia, one of Alexander VI's mistresses, was crowned pope with the title of Paul III. In his desire to create a duchy for his family, he gave Parma and Piacenza to his son, Pier Luigi. The Farneses reigned in Parma and Piacenza until 1731. Paul III's pontificate was further marked by important changes in the Church, all of which confirmed the spiritual autocracy of Rome. In 1540 he approved the foundation of the Jesuit order. The Inquisition was established with almost unlimited powers in Italy, and the press was placed under its jurisdiction. Free thought was shackled, to the profit of both ecclesiastical and political tyrants. Henceforth, it was impossible to publish or to utter any word which might offend the despots of church or state. In 1545 a council was opened at Trent for the reformation of Church discipline and the promulgation of orthodox doctrine. The decrees of this council defined Roman Catholicism against the Reformation. To outsiders, Italy appeared possessed of a hectic and hysterical piety. Meanwhile, at the core, Italy's clergy and aristocracy were more corrupt than ever.

Reign of Philip II

In 1556, when Charles V abdicated, his son Philip II became king of Spain — a domain he added to his kingdom of the Two Sicilies and his duchy of Milan. The following year his uncle, Ferdinand, the brother of Charles V, became emperor. Meanwhile, the French had not entirely abandoned their claims to Italy. Gian Pietro Caraffa, who was made pope in 1555 with the name of Paul IV, revived the ancient papal policy of leaning on the French and began by encouraging them to undertake the conquest of Naples. But their attempt proved to be useless when Philip defeated the French at St. Quentin and Gravelines. The Peace of Château Cambrésis, signed in 1559, left the Spanish monarch the undisputed lord of Italy. The only free commonwealths to survive were Venice, Genoa, and the two small republics of Lucca and San Marino.

Italy's future, however, was hidden in a remote and hitherto neglected corner of Europe. Emmanuel Philibert, Duke of Savoy, represented the oldest reigning house in Europe. His descendants would eventually establish independence for Italy — a feat no other power or prince had achieved since the fall of ancient Rome.

When Emmanuel Philibert succeeded his father in 1553, he was a duke without a duchy. But this would soon change on account of his association with his cousin, King Philip II of Spain. The Treaty of Château Cambrésis restored his possession of Savoy, and when the French evacuated Piedmont by moving his capital to Turin, its capital, the dukes of Savoy were transformed into Italian sovereigns. They now owned Savoy, beyond the Alps, the plains of Bresse, and the maritime province of Nice.

Emmanuel Philibert was succeeded by his son, Charles Emmanuel I, who married Catherine, daughter of Philip II. Now backed by the Spanish Crown, Charles Emmanuel I annexed Saluzzo, which had been lost to Savoy, and resumed his grandfather's disastrous policy by invading Geneva and threatening Provence. In 1601 Henry IV of France forced him to relinquish Bresse and his Burgundian possessions, but allowed him to keep Saluzzo. All attempts at conquests beyond the Alps were abandoned, but the keys to the kingdom of Italy had been given to the House of Savoy.

Extinction of the Old Ducal Families

Towards the end of the sixteenth century, several of the ancient ducal families began to dwindle. The legitimate Este line ended in 1597 with the death of Alfonso II, the last duke of Ferrara. He left his domain to his bastard son, Cesare d'Este, but Pope Urban VIII put in a claim to Ferrara and seized it for the papacy. Under the same pope, the papacy absorbed the duchy of Urbino upon the death of Francesco Maria II, the last representative of the Montefeltros and the Della Roveres. The popes were now masters of a fairly large territory. Meanwhile, Spanish fanaticism, the suppression of the Huguenots in France, and Austria's Catholic policy combined to strengthen the pontiff's authority. Urban VIII's successor, Paul V, went so far as to extend his spiritual jurisdiction to Venice, which up to 1605, the date of his election, had managed to fend off all encroachments of the Holy See.

The Decline of Venice and Spain

Venice rapidly declined throughout the seventeenth century. The loss of trade with the Levant, together with the discovery of America, had dried up its chief source of wealth. Venice's prolonged warfare with the Ottomans resulted in the loss of Candia in 1669, Cyprus in 1570, and crippled resources. By the eighteenth century, the Venetian nobles had abandoned themselves to indolence and vice. Many became paupers and were saved from starvation by the public dole. Though the signory made a brave show during parades, it was clear that the state had sunk into decrepitude.

Meanwhile, during the same epoch, the Spanish monarchy was also declining. Philip's Austrian successors had reduced Spain to a secondary European power. This decline was felt, concomitantly, in lower Italy. The revolt in Naples (1647), followed by rebellions in Palermo and Messina, were symptoms of progressive anarchy. The population, burdened by preposterous taxes, rose in exasperation against their oppressors. Yet these revolutions were of no significant political importance and did not bring the people any appreciable good. Italy's destiny was decided in the cabinets and on the battlefields of northern Europe.

This inglorious chapter in Italian history lasted until the French Revolution. Italy was handled and re-handled, settled and resettled, and changed masters during three dynastic wars of the period: the War of the Spanish Succession, the War of the Polish Succession, and the War of the Austrian Succession. These wars were followed by three European treaties, in which Italy was merely a pawn.

The Wars of Succession

In 1700 Charles II died, and this marked the end of the Austrian family in Spain. Louis XIV claimed the throne for Philip, Duke of Anjou, who was opposed by Charles, archduke of Austria. The dispute was fought in Flanders, and the French armies were defeated with the help of Prince Eugene of Savoy, who drove them out of Italy in 1707. According to the Treaty of Utrecht (1713), the House of Savoy had to be rewarded for its help; thus, Victor Amadeus II was given Sicily with the title of king.

The War of the Polish Succession is important in Italian history because the Treaty of Vienna (1738) settled the disputed affairs of the duchies of Parma and Tuscany. Don Carlos, Duke of Parma, took control of the Two Sicilies, while Francis of Lorraine, the husband of Maria Theresa, took Tuscany and Parma. Milan and Mantua remained in the hands of the Austrians.

There were worse implications for the Italians when Emperor Charles, the father of Maria Theresa, died in 1740. The three branches of the Bourbon house — who ruled in France, Spain, and the Sicilies — joined Prussia, Bavaria, and the kingdom of Sardinia (now belonging to the House of Savoy) to despoil Maria Theresa of her heritage. The War of the Austrian Succession followed, ending in 1748 with the Treaty of Aix-la-Chapelle. Italy was re-divided: Parma, Piacenza, and Gastalla were formed into a duchy for Don Philip, brother of Charles III of the Two Sicilies and son of Philip V of Spain; Charles III was confirmed in his kingdom of the Two Sicilies; the Austrians kept Milan and Tuscany; and the duchy of Modena was placed under the protection of the French, as was Genoa.

Forty-Four Years of Peace

Following the Treaty of Aix-la-Chapelle, from 1748 to 1792, Italy enjoyed a period of repose and an internal improvement of conditions under its numerous paternal despots. During these forty-four years of peace, it became fashionable to encourage the growth of industry and to experiment in economic reforms.

The Austrian government in Lombardy, under Maria Theresa, was characterized by improved agriculture, regular administration,

69

reformed taxation, and increased education. A considerable amount of local autonomy was allowed, while dependence on Vienna was slight and reasonable. The nobles and clergy were rich and influential, but they were kept in check by the civil power. Although there was not yet a feeling of nationality, the people were prosperous, enjoyed peace, and were generally content with the existing order of things.

After Maria Theresa's death in 1780, the emperor Joseph II instituted much wider reforms. Feudal privileges were done away with, clerical influence was diminished, and many monasteries and convents were suppressed. Criminal law became more humane, and torture was abolished. On the whole, the Austrian rule was beneficial and far from oppressive, helping Lombardy to recover from the ill effects of the Spanish domination. Emperor Francis I ruled the grand duchy of Tuscany until his death, when it was given to his second son, Peter Leopold. The reign of Leopold was one of internal prosperity, wise legislation, and important public enterprise. In 1790 he succeeded to the empire and turned Tuscany over to his son, Ferdinand.

During this period, the Jesuits made themselves odious — not only in Italy, but in France and Spain as well. Pope Clement XIV finally suppressed the Jesuit order altogether in 1773.

ITALY IN THE NAPOLEONIC PERIOD: 1796–1814

For many generations, Italy had been bandied about between the Hapsburgs and the Bourbons. The decline of French influence at the end of Louis XIV's reign left the Hapsburgs and the Spanish Bourbons without serious rivals. The former possessed the rich duchies of Milan, Mantua, and Tuscany, while, through a marriage alliance with the House of Este, its influence over the duchy of Modena was supreme. The Hapsburgs also had fiefs in Piedmont and in Genoese territory. By marrying her daughter, Maria Amelia, to the young duke of Parma and another daughter, Maria Carolina, to Ferdinand of Naples, Maria Theresa consolidated Hapsburg influence north and south of the peninsula. The Spanish Bourbons held Naples and Sicily, as well as the duchy of Parma.

Of the independent states, the principal one was the kingdom of Sardinia. It was ruled by the House of Savoy, which consisted of Piedmont, the isle of Sardinia and, nominally, Savoy and Nice.

Equally extensive, but less important in the political sphere, were the Papal States, torpid under the obscurantist rule of pope and cardinals, and Venice, enervated by luxury and complaisance. Genoa, Venice's rival, was likewise in decline. The small states of Lucca and San Marino completed the map of Italy. Poor government plagued the southern peninsula, where feudalism lay heavily on the cultivators and corruption pervaded all ranks. Milan and Piedmont were comparatively well governed, but repugnance of Austrian rule in Milan and the contagion of French Jacobinical opinions in Piedmont made the people increasingly hostile to their foreign masters.

The democratic propaganda that permeated the large towns of the peninsula led to the formation of numerous powerful clubs and secret societies. Meanwhile, the throne of Victor Amadeus III of the House of Savoy began to totter under the blows delivered by both the French troops at the mountain barriers of his kingdom and by the friends of liberty at Turin. Plotting was rife in Milan, as well as in Bologna. At Palermo, the Sicilians struggled to establish a republic in place of the decrepit government of an alien dynasty. The Grand Duke of Tuscany was the first of the European sovereigns to make peace with and recognize the French republic, early in 1795.

Bonaparte in Italy

The Napoleonic campaign of 1796 awakened the Italian people to a newfound unity and strength. The first fortnight of Napoleon's campaign severed Sardinia's alliance with Austria and England. The Italians' enthusiasm for the young Corsican "liberator" greatly helped Napoleon's progress. Two months later, Ferdinand of Naples sought an armistice, and the central duchies were easily overrun. Meanwhile, early in 1797, Pope Pius VI was ready to sign terms of peace with Napoleon at Tolentino, practically ceding the northern part of his states known as the Legations. The surrender of Mantua, the last Hapsburg stronghold, on February 2, 1797, opened the door to the implementation of new political institutions.

Napoleon's sortie into Italy began in the spring of 1796, when he led a French army over the Alps. He drove the Austrians from Lombardy, pushed into the Veneto, and "liberated" Bologna and the Romagna. In Emilia, local Jacobins rose up and forced out their duke. Napoleon's decisiveness and the speed of his victories left him free to act without seeking the permission of Paris. In northern Italy, he carved out two new states: the Cispadane and the Cisalpine republics. In October of the following year, he concluded his campaign by signing the Treaty of Campoformio, by which Venice was handed over to Austria and stripped of its status as an independent state. Napoleon left Italy in November, but his brief foray into the peninsula plunged France into a war of expansion and conquest, from which it would be unable to extricate itself.

In 1800 Napoleon crossed the Alps once more to reassert French power; this time, his victories led to a more permanent conquest. The next fifteen years consisted of political confusion in Italy, where boundaries were rubbed out and redrawn with such frequency that the people must have been unsure at any given moment exactly whose subjects they were. Some major changes to occur during this period include the following: the Cisalpine Republic was restored and made into the Italian Republic; Tuscany became the Kingdom of Etruria; Piedmont was annexed to France, together with Liguria, Parma, Umbria, and Lazio; and a Kingdom of Italy was set up in the north in 1805, with Milan as its capital. In addition, Naples was conquered by the French in 1806 and its Crown given to Napoleon's brother, Joseph. Two years later, it passed to Napoleon's brother-in-law, Joachim Murat.

Even Sicily and Sardinia, the two regions Napoleon had failed to conquer, lost some measure of autonomy. Sicily, where the Bourbon king had sought refuge in 1806, was occupied by a large British garrison. Sardinia, the home of the Savoy dynasty-in-exile, owed its independence largely to the vigilance of the British fleet.

But Napoleon over-extended himself and his resources. When his Russian campaign ended in defeat, he was deposed (1814) and sent into exile. The arrangements made by his enemies in accordance with the Treaty of Paris (June 12, 1814) and the Final Act of the Congress of Vienna (June 9, 1815) imposed boundaries on Italy, which resembled those of the pre-Napoleonic era.

France ceded its old provinces, Savoy and Nice, to the kingdom of Sardinia, now reconstituted under King Victor Emmanuel I. Great Britain and Austria insisted on the addition of the territories of the former republic of Genoa, which led King Victor Emmanuel to assume the title of Duke of Genoa. Austria recovered Milan and all possessions of the old Venetian Republic on the mainland, including Istria and Dalmatia. The Ionian Islands, formerly belonging to Venice, were placed under the protection of Great Britain by a treaty signed at Paris on November 5, 1815.

As a result of a treaty signed on April 24, 1815, the Austrian territories in northern Italy became the kingdom of Lombardo-Venetia, which, though an integral part of the Austrian empire, enjoyed a separate administration. Francis IV, son of Archduke Ferdinand of Austria and Maria Beatrice, daughter of Ercole Rinaldo, the last of the Este family, was reinstated as Duke of Modena. Parma and Piacenza were assigned to Marie Louise, daughter of the Austrian emperor and wife of Napoleon, on behalf of her son, the little Napoleon. But by a subsequent arrangement (1816–1817), the duchy was to revert at her death to the Bourbons of Parma, then reigning at Lucca. Tuscany was restored to Grand-Duke Ferdinand III of Hapsburg-Lorraine. The duchy of Lucca would return to Parma and be handed over to Tuscany.

Pope Pius VII, who had long been imprisoned by Napoleon at Fontainebleau, returned to Rome in May 1814 and was recognized by the Congress of Vienna as the sovereign of all former possessions of the Holy See. Ferdinand IV of Naples returned from Sicily to take possession of his dominions on the mainland. He received them back in their entirety, along with his new title, "Ferdinand I of the Two Sicilies."

IL RISORGIMENTO: 1815–1870

The dictionary defines *risorgimento* as a revival, rebirth, or awakening. *Il Risorgimento* is Italy's great national revival, which occurred in the middle of the nineteenth century. During this movement, all segments of society sought and finally achieved nationhood. Italy surged from the fragmentation it had suffered in the Middle Ages to successfully attain modernity and a respected place in the twentieth century. The *Risorgimento* is perhaps the most important period in Italy's history, for it led — step by painful step — to a democracy, developing economy, and a unified nation.

Austrian Rule in Italy

As a result of the Vienna treaties, Austria governed Lombardy and Venetia directly, and Austrian princes ruled in Modena, Parma, and Tuscany. Piacenza, Ferrara, and Comacchio had Austrian garrisons. Prince Metternich, the Austrian chancellor, believed that he could always secure the election of a pro-Austrian pope.

Austria also concluded offensive and defensive alliances with Sardinia, Tuscany, and Naples; Metternich's ambition was to make Austrian predominance over Italy still more absolute by placing an Austrian archduke on the Sardinian throne.

Reaction in the Italian States

Victor Emmanuel I, King of Sardinia, was the only native ruler in the peninsula, and the Savoy dynasty was popular throughout Italy. Emmanuel I's objective was to restore his dominions to the condition they were in before the French occupation. The French system of taxation was maintained because it brought in ample revenues; feudalism was revived, and all of the officers and officials who had served him before the Revolution were restored to their posts. Moreover, only nobles were eligible for the higher government appointments. Those who had served under the French administration were either dismissed or reduced in rank.

All this soon provoked discontentment among the educated classes. In Genoa, the government was particularly unpopular, as the Genoese resented being handed over to Piedmont, their old enemy. Nevertheless, the king disliked the Austrians and would have willingly seen them driven from Italy.

In Lombardy, French rule ended by making itself unpopular. Even before the fall of Napoleon, a national party called the *Italici puri* (pure Italians) had begun to advocate the independence of Lombardy.

In Modena, Duke Francis proved to be a cruel tyrant. In Parma, on the other hand, there was very little oppression, while

Lucca, too, enjoyed good government. The rule of Ferdinand and his minister, Fossombroni, in Tuscany was mild and benevolent, yet at the same time enervating and demoralizing.

The Papal States were ruled by a unique system of theocracy: Not only the head of state, but all the more important officials were ecclesiastics, assisted by the Inquisition, the Index, and all the paraphernalia of medieval church government. The administration was inefficient and corrupt, the censorship uncompromising, and the police oppressive.

In Naples, King Ferdinand retained some of the laws and institutions of Murat's regime, as well as many of the functionaries of the former government. But he revived the Bourbon tradition, the oppressive police system, and the censorship. A degrading religious bigotry became the basis of government and social life.

For centuries, Sicily enjoyed a feudal constitution, modernized and anglicized under British auspices in 1812. But the constitution was abolished in 1816, and the island was converted into a Neapolitan province governed by Neapolitan bureaucrats.

The oppression and follies of the restored government made people forget the evils of French rule and remember only its positive side; for, the French had breathed new life into the country, implementing improved laws, efficient administration, and the reform of old abuses. Meanwhile, the revival of national pride was a force to be reckoned with. Among the nobility and the educated middle classes, there developed either despair at Italy's moral degradation, as expressed in the writings of Foscolo and Leopardi, or a passion of hatred and revolt, manifested in the formation of secret societies.

The Carbonari

Carbonari, the Italian word for "charcoal burners," was the name of certain secret revolutionary societies which played an active part in the history of Italy and France early in the nineteenth century. During the reign of Joachim Murat (1808–1815), a number of secret societies arose with the objective of freeing the country from foreign rule and obtaining constitutional liberties. Their watchwords were "freedom" and "independence." There were several uprisings, all abortive, which involved the Carbonari — the two most notable being the revolts in Naples and in Piedmont. But, in both cases, the revolt was quashed by the Austrians.

During the next few years, order reigned in Italy except for a few insignificant outbreaks in the Papal States. But in 1823 Leo XII, a ferocious reactionary, became pope, and under his rule barbarous laws were enacted and torture frequently applied. The Carbonari and the other secret societies, the Adelfi and the Bersaglieri d'America, responded to these persecutions by assassinating the more brutal officials and spies. There was increased agitation in the Papal States, and in 1825 masses of people were condemned to death, imprisoned, or exiled.

Revolutions of 1830

The July revolution in Paris and the declaration of the new king, Louis Philippe, signified that France would not intervene in the internal affairs of other countries nor permit other powers to do so — a statement of policy aimed at the Austrians, who felt it their right and duty to interfere in Italian affairs. The French statement aroused great hope among Italy's oppressed, and it was the immediate cause of a revolution in Romagna and the Marches. In February 1831 these provinces raised the red, white, and green Italian flag and shook off the papal yoke with surprising ease.

At Parma, too, there was an outbreak, and the demand for a constitution was denied. In Modena, Menotti, the revolutionary leader, conceived the idea of a united Italian state under Duke Francis of Modena. But when Menotti was arrested, Biagio Nardi led an insurrection in his absence and had himself declared dictator. His cry of "Italy is one; the Italian nation, one sole nation" was in vain, for the Austrians intervened and silenced the rebellion. The former governments were re-established in Parma, Modena, and Romagna. Menotti and many other patriots were hanged.

The aforementioned movements seemed to prove that the masses were not yet ready for revolution. The idea of unity, although advocated by a few revolutionary leaders, was far from being widely accepted. On the other hand, it was clear that the despotic governments could not hold their own without the assistance of foreign bayonets.

Mazzini, Garibaldi, and Cavour

The stage was set. Italy was awaiting leadership. In a stroke of good fortune, it found not one man, but three. First came the visionary and utopian, Giuseppe Mazzini. His contemporaries were two equally forceful and extraordinary men: the activist, Giuseppe Garibaldi, and the statesman-strategist, Count Camillo di Cavour. It was a northern trio; Mazzini was a Genoese lawyer, Garibaldi was a sailor born in Nice, and Cavour was an aristocrat from Turin, capital of the kingdom of Sardinia, which consisted of Savoy, Piedmont, and the island of Sardinia. What these men shared was a self-sacrificing devotion to the cause of a united Italy. Otherwise, it would be hard to imagine three more dissimilar characters.

Giuseppe Mazzini (1805–1872)

Born on June 22, 1805, in Genoa, where his father was a practicing physician and a university professor, Mazzini studied law at the University of Genoa; but his natural bent was towards literature. He wrote a considerable number of literary essays, the first of which was on "Dante's love of country." At the same time, he became possessed with the idea that Italians "ought to struggle for liberty of country." He devoted himself completely to political thought and, accordingly, his literary articles became more suggestive of advanced political liberalism.

Having joined the Carbonari and quickly risen to one of the higher grades in its hierarchy, Mazzini was entrusted with a special secret mission to Tuscany. But he soon became dissatisfied with the organization and decided to form one of his own. The new society, whose aim was purely patriotic, was discovered by the Piedmontese authorities, and Mazzini was arrested and imprisoned in the fortress at Savona for about six months. When his sentence was found to be impracticable for lack of evidence, he was released; but with so many restrictions to his liberty, he decided to leave the country and move to Marseilles.

Giuseppe Mazzini (1805–1872).

After his release from prison, Mazzini drafted the aims of an organization that would soon become famous throughout Europe: *La Giovane Italia*, or Young Italy. Its publicly avowed aims were to liberate Italy from foreign and domestic tyranny and to unify the country under a republican form of government. The motto was "God and the People" — the banner bore on one side the words, "Unity and Independence," and on the other, "Liberty, Equality, and Humanity."

In April 1831 Charles Albert succeeded Charles Felix on the Sardinian throne. Towards the end of that year, Mazzini wrote the new king a letter, published in Marseilles, urging him to take the lead in the impending struggle for Italian independence. Clandestinely reprinted and rapidly circulated all over Italy, its bold and outspoken words produced a great sensation. The letter was so offensive to the Sardinian government that orders were issued for the immediate arrest and imprisonment of the author should he attempt to cross the frontier.

Towards the end of 1831 Mazzini's Young Italy *Manifesto* appeared, followed by his *Journal*, which, smuggled across the Italian frontier, had great success. Alarmed, the Sardinians called upon the French government to order Mazzini's withdrawal from Marseilles (1832). Mazzini remained in hiding for a few months, but ultimately fled to Switzerland. In 1832 he was involved in an abortive revolutionary movement which took place in the Sardinian army. Several executions occurred, and Mazzini was sentenced to death.

The same year, in Geneva, Mazzini launched *L'Europe Centrale*, a journal whose main objective was the emancipation of Savoy. He was chiefly responsible for organizing a large body of German, Polish, and Italian exiles in a planned armed invasion of the duchy. Mazzini accompanied the group when it crossed the frontier on February 1, 1834, but the attack broke down ignominiously without a shot being fired.

In April the *Young Europe* association "of men who believe in a future of liberty, equality, and fraternity for all mankind" was formed, also under Mazzini's influence. It was followed soon afterwards by *Young Switzerland*, whose aim was to form an Alpine confederation to include Switzerland, Tyrol, Savoy, and the rest of the Alpine chain. But, toward the end of 1836, the Swiss Diet exiled Mazzini, who fled to London the following January. There, he earned a meager living by writing articles on Italian literature and contemporary literary figures.

The leaders of the revolutionary outbreaks in Milan and Messina in early 1848 had been secretly corresponding with Mazzini. Their action brought him back to Italy, where, for a short time, he actually bore arms under Garibaldi preceding the reoccupation of Milan.

In the beginning of 1849 Mazzini was nominated a member of the short-lived provisional government of Tuscany, which was formed following the flight of the grand duke. After Pope Pius IX's withdrawal and Rome's proclamation as a republic, Mazzini was appointed a member of the Roman triumvirate with supreme executive power (March 23, 1849). However, due to events beyond his control, he resigned and fled to Switzerland.

In 1857 Mazzini was in Italy once more, participating in an aborted plot against Genoa, Leghorn, and Naples. Again, he was sentenced to death. But, determined to carry on, he returned to London where he founded a new journal, *Pensiero ed Azione* (Thought and Action). "I am but one voice crying *Action*," he wrote, "but the state of Italy cries for it too." Mazzini then wrote to Victor Emmanuel, urging him to put himself at the head of the movement for Italian unity.

In 1865, by way of protest against the still hovering death sentence under which he lay, Mazzini was elected by Messina as a delegate to the Italian parliament. But, feeling himself unable to take the oath of allegiance to the monarchy, he never took the seat. The following year, his death sentence was at last removed. The remainder of Mazzini's life, spent partly in London and partly in Lugano, was uneventful. His health had not been good for some time, and an attack of pleurisy brought about his death at Pisa on March 10, 1872.

The Italian parliament acquitted itself with decency when, by unanimous vote, it expressed national sorrow over Mazzini's death. The president pronounced an eloquent eulogy on the departed patriot, hailing him as a model of patriotism and self-denial — a man who had dedicated his life ungrudgingly to the cause of his country's freedom. A public funeral took place at Pisa on March 14, and his remains were sent to Genoa.

Giuseppe Garibaldi (1807–1882)

Giuseppe Garibaldi was born in Nice on July 4, 1807. As a young man, he first joined the *Giovane Italia* (Italian Youth) and then entered the Sardinian navy. After being assigned to the frigate *Euridice*, with a number of companions on board, Garibaldi plotted to seize the vessel and occupy the arsenal at Genoa — just as Mazzini's Savoy expedition was expected to enter Piedmont. But Garibaldi fled when the plot was discovered and was condemned to death (June 3, 1834). His career as a born rebel was thus launched, and he was well on his way to liberating Italy.

Giuseppe Garibaldi (1807–1882).

Escaping to South America in 1836, Garibaldi took part in Rio Grande do Sul's revolt against Brazil. After a number of victorious engagements, he was taken prisoner and subjected to severe torture, from which he suffered dislocated limbs. When he regained his liberty, he returned to the war against Brazil and seized the port city of Porto Alegre. During the campaign, he met his wife, Anita, who became his inseparable companion and the mother of his three children, Anita, Ricciotti, and Menotti.

Meanwhile, the Argentine dictator, Juan Manuel de Rosa, whose imperialistic intention was to reduce Paraguay and Uruguay to dependent Argentine states, had moved against Uruguay. Always ready to defend the underdog, Garibaldi joined the Uruguayan forces and, with a small fleet, was sent to Corrientes to oppose Rosa's forces. He fought against a powerful fleet for three days; when his ammunition was exhausted, he burned his ships and escaped. Returning to Montevideo, he formed the Italian Legion, with which he won two battles in the spring of 1846, thereby assuring Uruguay's freedom.

Refusing all honors and recompense, Garibaldi returned to Italy upon receiving word of the incipient revolutionary movement. In October 1847 he wrote to Pius IX, offering his services to the Church, whose cause he then thought was national liberty.

Landing at Nice on June 24, 1848, Garibaldi placed himself at the disposal of Charles Albert. After various difficulties with the Piedmontese war office, Garibaldi was able to form a volunteer army of three thousand. But, defeated by the Austrians at Custozza, near Verona, he was obliged to flee to Switzerland. Like Mazzini, Garibaldi's life had become one of organized rebellion and flight to safety.

From Switzerland, Garibaldi went on to Rome, where the Roman republic entrusted him with its defense against the French. After remaining all day in the saddle and despite being wounded at the beginning of the battle, he won a victory at San Pancrazio on April 30, 1849.

From the third of May to the thirtieth, Garibaldi battled the Bourbon troops at the Roman communes of Palestrina and Velletri, where he dispersed an army of twenty thousand with only three thousand volunteers.

But when Rome fell, Garibaldi led four thousand volunteers out of the city, with the idea of joining the defenders of Venice. Thus, a spectacular retreat through central Italy began, pursued by the armies of France, Austria, Spain, and Naples. By his consummate generalship and the matchless endurance of his men, he managed to evade his pursuers and reach San Marino in central Italy — but with a sadly diminished force. Garibaldi and a few followers, including his devoted wife Anita, took refuge in the pine forests of Ravenna after vainly attempting to reach Venice. The Austrians were in hot pursuit and most of his legionaries were captured and shot.

Anita died near Comacchio, near the commune of Ferrara, and Garibaldi fled across the peninsula to Tuscany, then to Piedmont, and finally to America. In New York, in order to earn a living, he became first a chandler and then a trading skipper. Having made a small fortune, he returned to Italy in 1854 and purchased the island of Caprera, on which he built the house that became his permanent home.

But Garibaldi was never far from the battlefield. At the outbreak of war in 1859, he was placed in command of the Alpine Infantry, defeating the Austrians at Casale, a Piedmontese commune. Crossing the Ticino River between Italy and Switzerland on May 8, he liberated the Alpine territory as far as the frontier of the Tyrol, in the Italian Alto Adige, north of Venice. Garibaldi was about to enter Austrian territory, when his advance was checked by the armistice at Villafranca.

1860

Garibaldi returned to Como to wed Countess Raimondi, who had aided him during the campaign. But, apprised of another crisis, he abandoned her immediately after the wedding and took off for central Italy. Forbidden to invade the Romagna, he returned indignantly to Caprera, where he planned the invasion of Sicily with Crispi, a Sicilian patriot and statesman.

Assured of British protection, Garibaldi began active preparations for the expedition to Marsala. At the last moment he hesitated, but Crispi succeeded in persuading him to sail from Genoa on May 5, 1860, with two vessels carrying a volunteer corps of 1,070. Garibaldi landed at Marsala on May 11, under the protection of two British vessels, the *Intrepid* and *Argus*.

On May 12, Garibaldi's dictatorship was proclaimed at Salemi, in the province of Trapani; on May 15, the Neapolitan troops were routed at Calatafimi, also in Trapani; on May 25, Palermo fell; and on June 6, twenty thousand Neapolitan regulars, supported by nine frigates and protected by two forts, were forced to capitulate.

Once established in Palermo, Garibaldi organized an army to liberate Naples and march to Rome — a plan opposed by Lafarina and Depretis, representatives of Cavour, who desired the immediate annexation of Sicily to the Italian kingdom. In response, Garibaldi expelled them and went on to rout the Neapolitans at Milazzo, near Messina, on July 20. Messina itself fell on the same day, but Garibaldi, instead of crossing to Calabria, secretly sailed for Sardinia. Cavour, however, obliged him to change course and return to Messina.

At Messina, Garibaldi found a letter from Victor Emmanuel II, dissuading him from invading the kingdom of Naples. Garibaldi replied, asking for "permission to disobey." Thus, the next day he crossed the Strait, won the Battle of Reggio (Calabria) on August 21, and accepted the capitulation of nine thousand Neapolitan troops at San Giovanni (a commune in the province of Cosenza) and eleven thousand more at Soveria. The Calabrians later named a peak at Aspromonte, a high ridge in the southern Apennines, Mount Garibaldi, in his honor.

Garibaldi then led a triumphal march on to Naples, which King Francesco was powerless to stop. He entered Naples on September 7, while Francesco fled to Gaeta, the fortified seaport. On October 1, Garibaldi routed the remnants of the Bourbon army of forty thousand strong. Meanwhile, Italian troops had occupied the Marches, Umbria, and the Abruzzi, freeing a battalion of Bersaglieri (the sharpshooting troops) to reach the Volturno in time to take part in the battle. Their presence put an end to Garibaldi's plan to invade the Papal States; unwillingly, he issued a decree ordering the incorporation of the kingdom of the Two Sicilies into the Italian realm. On November 7, he accompanied King Victor Emmanuel in his solemn entry into Naples. The following day, Garibaldi returned to Caprera, after disbanding his volunteers and recommending that they join the regular Italian army.

1861

Indignant at the cession of Nice to France and the Italian government's neglect of his followers, Garibaldi decided to return to political life. Elected deputy in 1861, his anger against Cavour found violent expression. In particular, a published letter by General Enrico Cialdini, commander of Victor Emmanuel's troops, against Garibaldi provoked a hostility which, but for the intervention of the king, would have led to a duel between Cialdini and Garibaldi. Returning to Caprera, Garibaldi awaited events.

That same year, Cavour died and was succeeded by Bettino Ricasoli, who enrolled the Garibaldians in the regular Italian army. Ricasoli, in turn, was succeeded by Urbano Rattazzi, who urged Garibaldi to undertake an expedition in aid of the Hungarians. Garibaldi, finding his followers ill-disposed toward the idea, decided instead to turn his arms against Rome.

1862–1882

Landing at Palermo on June 29, 1862, Garibaldi gathered an army under the banner *Roma o morte,* "Rome or death." Rattazzi, frightened at the prospect of an attack on Rome, proclaimed a state of siege in Sicily, sent the fleet to Messina, and instructed Cialdini to oppose Garibaldi.

Circumventing the Italian troops, Garibaldi entered Catania on August 25 and crossed to Melito in Calabria with three thousand men. But he was wounded in the ankle and taken prisoner by Cialdini's forces at Aspromonte two days later. Freed by amnesty, he returned to Caprera amidst general sympathy.

In Caprera, Garibaldi matured his plans against Rome. Gathering volunteers in the autumn of 1867, he prepared to enter papal territory, but was arrested at Sinalunga in Tuscany by the Italian government. He was conducted to Caprera, where he remained for a short time.

In 1870 Garibaldi formed a fresh volunteer corps and went to the aid of France, defeating the German troops at Chatillon, Autun, and Dijon. Elected a member of the Versailles assembly, he resigned his mandate, angered by French insults, and withdrew once more to Caprera until, in 1874, he was elected deputy for Rome.

Popular enthusiasm induced the Conservative government to propose that Garibaldi be given the sum of forty thousand liras and an annual pension of two thousand liras, as recompense for his services to Italy. The proposal (May 27, 1875) was indignantly refused by Garibaldi, but later accepted when the Left was returned to power. At the same time, after having his marriage to Countess Raimondi annulled, he contracted another marriage with the mother of his two children, Clelia and Manlio.

In 1880 Garibaldi went to Milan for the inauguration of a monument at Mentana, where many of his troops had been killed and captured. In 1882 he visited Naples and Palermo, but illness prevented him from being present at the 600TH anniversary of the Sicilian Vespers. On June 2, 1882, his death at Caprera plunged Italy into mourning.

Giuseppe Garibaldi lived for seventy-five years, and with the exception of his early years devoted much of his life to Italy's unification and freedom. He has a firm place in history as his country's hero and as the hero of the *Risorgimento*. He had the courage, dedication, and selflessness to wage war against Italy's enemy — and against all the enemies of freedom and liberty.

Count Camillo Benso di Cavour (1810–1861)

Conte di Cavour (1810–1861).

If Mazzini was the prophet of Italian unity, and Garibaldi its knight errant, then Cavour deserves the honor of having been the statesman by whom it was finally accomplished.

Cavour was born in Turin on August 1, 1810, the son of two noble families. The Bensos, who belonged to the old Piedmontese feudal aristocracy, were an ancient house said to have descended from a Saxon warrior who married a Piedmontese heiress. Cavour's father, the Marquis Michele, married a noble Genovese lady and both he and his wife served Prince Borghese, the governor of Piedmont under Napoleon.

As a younger son, Cavour was destined for the army; at age ten, he entered the military academy at Turin. When he left the academy, he spent the next five years in the army, devoting many hours to study, especially of the English language. He also developed marked liberal tendencies and a dislike for absolutism and clericalism. He resigned his commission in 1831, and from that moment on thought of himself as an opponent of the government.

Cavour's political ideas were greatly influenced by the French Revolution of July 1830 — an event which proved that a historic monarchy was not incompatible with liberal principles. He became more than ever convinced of the benefits of a constitutional monarchy, as opposed to despotism and republicanism.

In tune with the French and British political ideas of the time, Cavour began to dream of a united Italy, free of foreign influence. But owing to the reactionary policy of the Piedmontese government, he was unable to take any active part in politics.

In 1847, however, the moment seemed to have arrived; for, the new pope, Pius IX, showed marked liberal tendencies and seemed ready to lead all the forces of Italian patriotism against the Austrian domination. Cavour took the first positive action toward unification by founding a newspaper in Turin, *Il Risorgimento*. This newspaper advocated constitutional reform in Piedmont, with the aim of preparing it for an important role in the upheaval which seemed imminent.

In January of the following year, revolution first broke out in Sicily. In a speech before a delegation of journalists, Cavour declared that the king must grant his people a constitution. Strong pressure was brought to bear on King Charles Albert and, after much hesitation, he was persuaded to grant a charter of liberties (February 8, 1848). Cesare Balbo, one of the proponents of a constitutional monarchy, was called upon to form the first constitutional ministry. Cavour, who had not been offered a seat in the ministry, continued to write articles for *Il Risorgimento*.

When news of the Milanese revolt against the Austrians reached Turin on March 19, Cavour felt that the time for Piedmont to act with energy had come and he advocated war against Austria. "After deliberately weighing each word," he wrote, "we are bound in conscience to declare that only one path is open to the nation, the government, and the king: war, immediate war!"

Piedmont was the only part of Italy which enjoyed a government that was both national and independent. It was felt that if Piedmont did not go to the assistance of the Milanese in their desperate struggle against the Austrians, then the monarchy could not survive. In an article in *Il Risorgimento*, Cavour stated his belief that while Piedmont could expect no help from England, the British would surely not actively help Austria crush the revolution. The article made such an impression on the king that it put an end to his vacillations. A few days after its appearance, on March 25, war was declared against Austria.

In all parts of Italy, too, revolts broke out against the established order; but the Piedmontese army, no match for the Austrian veteran legions, was generally unsuccessful. The revolts were brought to an end when an armistice was signed in the summer of 1848.

Meanwhile, elections were being held in Piedmont, and Cavour was elected to Parliament, taking his seat on the Right as a Conservative. It is ironic that the man who fought to create an Italian nation in fact had no command of the Italian language; for, French was Cavour's native tongue, and the speeches he wrote had to be translated into Italian before he could deliver them.

When the armistice was about to expire, King Charles Albert decided on a last desperate plunge and recommenced hostilities. After the Piedmontese were defeated at Novara on March 23, 1849, the king abdicated in favor of his son, Victor Emmanuel II.

Although the new king was obliged to conclude peace with Austria, and the Italian revolution was crushed, Cavour did not despair. He believed that as long as the constitution was maintained in Piedmont, the Italian cause was safe. He was returned to Parliament in the July election. In a speech on March 7, 1850, he stated: "Piedmont, gathering to itself all the living forces of Italy, will soon be in a position to lead our mother-country to the high destinies to which she is called." Cavour's statement struck an optimistic note after the dark days of the previous year.

In October of the same year, Cavour was named minister of agriculture, industry, and commerce, and in 1851 assumed the finance portfolio. A political maneuver, made without the knowledge or approval of Prime Minister d'Azeglio, led to his resignation. Cavour made use of his freedom to visit England, where he was assured that if the constitutional experiment in Piedmont succeeded, Italian despotism would be doomed.

On his return to Piedmont, Cavour found the country in the throes of a new cabinet crisis. Consequently, he was invited to form a cabinet. On November 4, he was appointed prime minister — a position he held, with only two short interruptions, until his death.

Cavour's first international difficulty was with Austria, which, after the abortive uprising in Milan in February 1853, had imposed measures of repression and confiscated the estates of the Lombards who declared themselves to be Piedmontese citizens. Cavour objected strongly to this decree. When Austria refused to rescind it, he took the bold step of recalling the Piedmontese minister to Vienna.

Cavour's goal continued to be the expulsion of Austria from Italy and the unification of the country under one flag. He understood that he must have Napoleon's cooperation to achieve both ends, so he arranged a meeting with the emperor in July 1858, during which the basis of an agreement was laid. France and Piedmont were to declare war against Austria with the object of expelling her from Italy, and a north Italian state was to be formed. In exchange for this help, France was to receive Savoy and Nice. Cavour also understood that in order to achieve unity throughout the country, he had to secure the cooperation of volunteers from other parts of Italy. This way, the war would truly be a national uprising against Austria and the local despots.

The moment war was seen as imminent, Italians of all classes, especially the Lombards, poured into Piedmont to enlist in the army. Cavour had a secret interview with Garibaldi, and together they organized a well-balanced volunteer corps of Piedmontese and Italians.

On January 10, 1859, the king, in a speech from the throne, pronounced the memorable words: "We cannot remain deaf to the cry of pain (*il grido di dolore*) that reaches us from all parts of Italy." These words rang out like a trumpet call throughout the land.

On April 23, Austria sent an ultimatum demanding the disarmament of Piedmont. Cavour replied that his government refused to do so. France now securely allied itself with Piedmont, and England, enraged by Austria's ultimatum, became sympathetic to the Italian cause. A few days later, Austria declared war.

When General La Marmora took command of the army, Cavour added the ministry of war to the other positions he already held. Now he was virtually dictator and single-handedly controlled nearly all the chief offices of state. The French troops entered Piedmont, where they were received with enthusiasm, and the allies marched into Lombardy. Their first victory was at Magenta, which ceded Milan to them.

Parma, Modena, Florence, and Bologna, which had been occupied by Austria for the pope since 1849, rose up in arms. Local princes were expelled and provisional governments were established. Cavour sent special commissioners to take charge of the various provinces in Victor Emmanuel's name.

But Cavour was thunderstruck when Napoleon, fearing that a large and powerful Italian state would be created, decided to pull out. Cavour implored the king not to make peace until Venice was free, but Victor Emmanuel went ahead and signed the peace preliminaries at Villafranca. Lombardy was to be ceded to Piedmont, Venice was to remain Austrian, the deposed princes were to be reinstated, and the pope was to be made president of an Italian confederation.

The cabinet resigned the next day, and Cavour privately advised the revolutionists of central Italy to resist the return of the princes, by force if necessary: "For we must now become conspirators, ourselves." Cavour's policy was continued after he left office. But he was not out of office long, for the king needed him badly; by January 1860, he was again prime minister, as well as minister of foreign affairs and the interior.

Cavour's first act was to invite the people of Italy to declare their own wishes with regard to the annexation of Piedmont. There were plebiscites of central Italy which unanimously favored the union with Piedmont. On March 24, a treaty was signed, and Napoleon's objection to the annexation of central Italy was withdrawn. On April 2, the parliament representing Piedmont, the duchies of Parma and Modena, Tuscany, and Romagna ratified the agreement by a large majority.

The situation in the kingdom of Naples was becoming critical, for the Bourbons were still in control and there seemed little chance of a union with upper Italy. But Cavour, having learned that Garibaldi was planning an expedition to Sicily with his volunteers, decided, after some hesitation, not to oppose its departure. On May 5, Garibaldi sailed from Quarto, near Genoa, landing at Marsala with his Immortal Thousand. The corrupt Bourbon government collapsed before the charge of this handful of volunteers, who soon occupied the entire island and proclaimed their leader Dictator of Sicily.

Garibaldi now crossed the Straits of Messina and began his march on Naples. Cavour had meanwhile taken a bold step, deciding to annex the Papal States with the exception of the Roman province. The Italian army crossed the frontier from Romagna on September 11 and the people received them with open arms. On October 1, Garibaldi defeated the Neapolitan troops and became Dictator of Naples.

But there were difficulties with Garibaldi, for he would not resign his dictatorship of the southern provinces; moreover, he was determined to march on Rome. Cavour had to use all of his tact to restrain him — yet, at the same time, he did not want to appear ungrateful. Preferring not to act despotically, he summoned Parliament to vote on the annexation of the south, which it did on October 11. Two days later, Garibaldi magnanimously gave in to the nation's will, handing his conquests over to King Victor as a free gift. Victor Emmanuel was proclaimed King of Italy.

Cavour's last obstacle was Rome. For some years, the pope had only been able to maintain his authority over a sizable part of central Italy with the help of foreign troops. Cavour recognized that as long as this state of affairs lasted, Italy could not be united. In October he declared to Parliament that Rome must be the capital of Italy, for no other city was recognized as such by the whole country. In January 1861 a resolution to that effect was passed.

At the same time, Cavour was anxious that the Church should preserve the fullest liberty, as he believed in the principle of "a free church in a free state." His great dream, save for Rome and Venice, was now realized: Italy was free and united.

But the wear and tear of these last years was at last taking its toll. Negotiations with Garibaldi were especially trying; although he wanted to treat the hero and his volunteers generously, he could not permit all the Garibaldian officers to be received into the regular army with the same grades they had held in the volunteer forces. This question, plus Garibaldi's resentment that Cavour had given Nice, his birthplace, away to the French, led to a painful scene between the two men. Cavour had been unwell and irritable for some time, and the scene with Garibaldi undoubtedly hastened his end. A fever set in, and he died shortly afterwards on June 6, 1861. Cavour was buried at his ancestral castle of Santena.

Cavour's death was a terrible loss to Italy. There remained many unsolved problems for which his genius and personality were urgently needed. But his great work had been carried to such a point that other men might now ably complete the structure. Cavour remains the greatest figure of the *Risorgimento*. Although other men and forces cooperated in the movement, it was Cavour who organized it and skillfully conducted the negotiations which overcame all obstacles. Cavour's one absorbing passion was the liberation and regeneration of Italy, and to this end he devoted his whole life and talent. His name completes the triumvirate of heroes of the *Risorgimento* — Mazzini, Garibaldi, and Cavour.

There was Prose, Poetry, and Music, Too

Three creative artists stand out during the *Risorgimento*: Leopardi, a great Italian poet; Manzoni, an outstanding Italian novelist; and Verdi, the supreme Italian composer.

Giacomo Leopardi (1798–1837)

Born at Recanati, south of Ancona, Giacomo Leopardi, an invalid, was educated at home. From an early age, he immersed himself in classical studies and became an accomplished scholar and philologist. He was a Romantic poet, concerned with the fallen state of his beloved Italy. Much of his poetry gave a voice to Italy's forlorn and degraded condition and its political impotence. Leopardi's *Ode to Italy* was the desperate cry of a lyrical poet: "Oh Fatherland, I see the towers of our forefathers/ But I do not see the glory [of] ancient times."

Alessandro Manzoni (1785–1873)

I promessi sposi (The Betrothed), one of the world's greatest historical novels, established Manzoni as the leading Italian romantic novelist of the nineteenth century. It is a work which raised Italian fiction from the low state to which it had fallen, to a high place in European fiction. In effect, Manzoni brought the Italian language forward into the modern world from the first steps taken by Dante and his contemporaries. Though it was not an overt propaganda novel, it spoke directly to emergent Italian patriotism.

I promessi sposi focused on events in Lombardy in the first half of the seventeenth century — a time when the people were being oppressed by their Spanish overlords. But Manzoni's nineteenth-century readers were capable of making the transposition to the Italy of their own day, as they too were suffering under the Austrians.

Giuseppe Verdi (1813–1901)

In May 1873 Alessandro Manzoni, one of Verdi's heroes, died in Milan at the age of eighty-nine. "Now it is all over," said Verdi, "and with him ends the most pure, the most holy, the greatest of our glories." Verdi then composed a Requiem Mass, which was performed on the first anniversary of Manzoni's death. With a chorus of one hundred and twenty voices and an orchestra of one hundred, the performance was an enormous success, and the Requiem passed into history as one of the great masterpieces of Italian music.

Verdi was twenty-six when he embarked on a career as a composer of opera. Until age eighty, he wrote some twenty-five operas, most of which are acclaimed masterpieces: *Rigoletto* (1851), *Il Trovatore* (1853), *La Traviata* (1853), *Un Ballo in Maschera* (1859), *La Forza del Destino* (1862), *Don Carlos* (1867), and *Aida* (1871). He was fifty-eight when he composed *Aida*, and everyone assumed that this was his last opera. How could anyone possibly produce an opera in old age? But Verdi did, sixteen years later, at age seventy-one; and twenty-two years later, at age eighty, he composed his finest operas based on Shakespeare — *Otello* (1887) and *Falstaff* (1893).

Giuseppe Verdi (1813–1901).

If Mazzini, Cavour, and Garibaldi heralded and established Italy's freedom and unification, and if Leopardi and Manzoni forged its poetry and language, then Verdi, the sixth hero of the *Risorgimento*, was the giant who capped the movement with some of the finest music written anywhere, anytime.

Certainly, there were other composers, to mention but two. The first was Gioacchino Rossini, whose comic *Barber of Seville* (1816) electrified Europe and made its composer more famous than Beethoven. The second was a Sicilian, Vincenzo Bellini (1801–1835), composer of *Norma* (1831), *La sonnambula* (1831), and *I Puritani* (1835).

FORGING A MODERN ITALY: 1871–1920

The latter 1800s were a difficult period for Italy as it approached the twentieth century. To begin with, there were social, economic, and agricultural problems to be solved. The south —the land below Rome, plus Sicily and Sardinia — had been neglected and misused by greedy lords and rulers. The last of these rulers was the Spanish House of Bourbon, which was so corrupt that with a mere handful of ill-equipped volunteers, Garibaldi was able to topple an army of some thirty thousand troops in a matter of days. They wore shiny uniforms, but there was no patriotism, incentive, or strength beneath the cloth. The south would continue to be neglected right into the twentieth century.

At about the same time as the American Civil War, there was also a civil war between the north and south in Italy. Naples, which had recently rebelled against Bourbon misgovernment, chafed under the colonial rule of the north. Brigands often set upon the highly unpopular "carpetbaggers." Thus, the war was partly an insurrection in the south, and partly a northern campaign of retaliation against southern brigandage.

The oppressed peasants of the south, disillusioned with the failure of the government to bring them justice, regarded the brigands as their champions in their struggle against the landlords. These outlaws were even accepted by the Church and the unseated Bourbons.

The government sent an army of 120,000 into the south. When the civil war was over, it was found that the number of people who had died was greater than the total number killed in the wars of the *Risorgimento*. Brigandage survived and flourished. In Sicily, it was personified in the Mafia — a group of gangs who extorted protection money and presided over smuggling and kidnapping activities; in Naples, it was manifested in the Camorra, which specialized in intimidation and blackmail, organized its own police force and courts of justice, and sometimes placed its own deputies in Parliament.

When Rome became the capital of Italy, the pope lost his temporal powers. The result was the beginning of a long and vexing struggle between the Vatican and the Italian government. The pope rejected the compensations offered him by the government, refused to recognize the existence of the Italian state, and voluntarily "imprisoned" himself in the Vatican.

In the south, millions lived in a state of absolute want, deprived of foodstuffs and housed in hovels, lean-tos, and even caves. Education was sadly neglected; the tradition of education had not died, but now it was confined to the upper strata of society. Teachers were underpaid and, very often, not paid at all.

Yet the Italian laborers were some of the hardest working in the world. Because there was insufficient employment at home, they traveled to other countries to help build the Suez Canal, the harbor of Marseilles, and the railroads and cities of North and South America. In the first fifteen years of the new century, some four million people left southern Italy to work abroad, principally in the United States. They were attracted by the high wages to be had in American factories and on construction sites, and by the increasingly cheap transatlantic fares.

The Triple Alliance

In 1882, piqued by France's annexation of Tunisia — a country the Italians had long coveted — Italy joined Prussia and Austria in concluding the Triple Alliance.

Francesco Crispi (1818–1901)

Italy soon embarked on a ruinous race for armaments, colonies, and prestige. It was under the iron rule of Premier Francesco Crispi that Italy began a tariff war with France, which bankrupted its economy. Undaunted, Crispi decided that only the conquest of Ethiopia would free Italy from its "imprisonment in the Mediterranean," fulfill its "mission" in Africa, and detract attention from the corrupt nature of its regime. A mismanaged military campaign resulted in a humiliating defeat at Aduwa in 1896. Italy was stunned, and Crispi fell from power.

Four years later, in 1900, the unpopular King Umberto was assassinated. His son, Vittorio Emanuele III, was a more sober king than his father. Emanuele III was fortunate to have at his side a reformer from Piedmont, Giovanni Giolitti, who served as premier for most of the period between 1901 and 1914.

Giovanni Giolitti (1842–1928)

Giovanni Giolitti was a bureaucrat who, by hard work and genuine ability, had risen to the highest post in the civil service. Giolitti's government was liberal, and as such was opposed by the Socialists; but the premier stole their thunder by absorbing most of their agenda into current legislation, without ever adopting their political principles. Giolitti's clever and unscrupulous handling of parties preserved his majority and enabled him to carry out a long list of valuable social legislation. But his methods sapped parliamentary life of virility and deprived large sections of the electorate of all interest in politics.

Giolitti's most notable achievement was his attempt to meet the growing social unrest in Italy with concessions rather than repression. He believed that Italy could achieve stability only by giving the working class a greater stake in the nation's prosperity. Unlike his predecessors, Giolitti encouraged labor unions instead of persecuting them. He greatly extended the franchise, thereby making way for new mass parties — Socialist, Fascist, and Church-backed — to develop. Italy prospered; foreign trade doubled between 1900 and 1910, wages increased, and the standard of living improved. Even the southern question became less acute for the moment — not because conditions in the south had improved, but because surplus agricultural labor was now emigrating.

In 1912 Italian morale was boosted at last by colonial success. A year-long war in Libya against the Turks and the Arabs ended in an Italian victory and the establishment of a Colonies Ministry. But while it gave Italy a toehold in Africa, the triumph was an expensive one. Capital was needed to develop the new colony, and Italy did not even have enough to develop its own land.

End of the Triple Alliance

Italy began to move away from the Triple Alliance when Austria and Germany invaded Serbia without consulting their third partner. When World War I broke out, Italy felt free, therefore, to announce its neutrality (August 2, 1914). The Italian foreign secretary then informed Vienna that the only territory Italy would accept was that situated in the Italian provinces held by Austria, the Trentino. Austria refused even to discuss the matter.

Italy Moves Toward War

When a last attempt to induce Austria to satisfy Italy's share in the Balkans was met with stark refusal, Salandra, who followed Giolitti as premier, turned to England and France. Negotiations were begun and, on April 26, 1915, a secret treaty with the Allies was signed. The terms were all that Italy could ask for; it was to have the Trentino and a defensive frontier on the Brenner Pass, Trieste and Istria, part of the Dalmatian coast, the port of Valona, special rights in Albania, Rhodes and the Dodecanese, and certain islands in the Adriatic. In May, Italy publicly announced its withdrawal from the Triple Alliance.

Italy at War: 1915–1918

Italy was utterly unprepared for war, with its deficiency in funds and in the modern implements of combat, including munitions and heavy artillery. Moreover, the army was top-heavy with colonels and generals, and possessed few lieutenants and captains. Italy's entry into war in May 1915, as an ally of the French and British, ended in disaster. In its first two offensives, Italy lost a quarter of a million men.

In the spring of 1916 the Austrians launched an attack in the Gorizia region. Fighting in the summer in the dry limestone hills of the Carso proved grim and costly for both sides; and summer was followed by a severe winter along the whole mountainous front.

In 1917 the tide turned against Italy. In October, German divisions reinforced a massive Austrian offensive on the Isonzo front. The Italian line crumbled, and with it the morale of the troops.

A final spring offensive by Austria on the Piave in 1918 met with total failure; but in the autumn, the Italians and their allies sealed a victory in the Battle of Vittorio Veneto. On November 4, an armistice was signed between Austria and Italy, one week before the armistice on the Western Front. In the three years and six months of fighting, Italy mobilized 5.2 million men, of whom 680,000 were killed.

When it came to dividing up the booty, Italy was treated as a junior partner. The negotiations in Paris gave Italy a vast tract of desert in the Libyan hinterlands, and a tiny extension of Italian Somaliland in East Africa.

The question of Fiume was not resolved for another year. According to the allied Treaty of London, Italy was to receive Fiume, with its almost entirely Italian population, and Dalmatia. But President Woodrow Wilson, who forged the Fourteen Points, seemed unaware of the London treaty and insisted that Fiume and Dalmatia go to Croatia.

While Wilson's defeat in the American elections of 1918 robbed Yugoslavia of its chief advocate, Italy still did not receive these two key cities. On November 12, 1920, by the Treaty of Rapallo, a settlement was finally reached. Italy was to have the Istrian peninsula, and Yugoslavia was to have Dalmatia. Fiume was declared a free state, along with a strip of coastline which connected it to Italy's Istrian peninsula. By the Treaty of 1947, Fiume eventually became part of Croatia.

THE DARK AGE OF FASCISM: 1920–1945

Benito Mussolini (1883–1945)

Born in 1883 of a peasant family in the small village of Predappio in the Romagna, Benito was named after the Mexican revolutionary, Benito Suárez. Mussolini's father was the local blacksmith, whose smithy was the center for the local proponents of the Russian Bakunin's Anarchist-Socialist philosophy, a branch of which was established at nearby Forlì in 1874.

Anarchism sought equality and justice through the abolition of the state, capitalism, and private property. Bakunin attempted to orient the First International towards anarchism, but was defeated by Marx. It was Bakunin who gave modern anarchism its collectivist and violent tone. The Bolsheviks suppressed political anarchism in Russia after the Russian Revolution.

But anarchism was a real force among the peasants of the Romagna, who were in revolt against the bitter treatment of the great landowners, the municipalities, and the government. Despite the government's oppressive action, handing out long prison sentences for "sedition" and "conspiracy," anarchist-socialism prospered and spread. Mussolini's father became the leader of the local Socialist group.

Young Mussolini was immersed at home in the violent political philosophy of nihilistic anarchism. Though it took many sudden turns, essentially this was the philosophy that motivated him throughout his career, right up to his ignominious death. He was fundamentally anti-government — a political stance which lies at the heart of Fascism.

After spending a year as an elementary school teacher, Mussolini went to Switzerland, where he remained from the middle of 1902 until the spring of 1904. There, he lived in dire poverty, barely earning a living as a bricklayer and mason. To his hatred of proprietors he added an almost hysterical hatred of the well-groomed, polite young Socialists from the middle classes.

From masonry, Mussolini went on to work as a clerk in a wine shop. In his spare time, he attended lectures at the University of Lausanne. He also frequented Socialist and Anarchist clubs

Benito Mussolini, as Make-believe Conqueror.

organized by Russian refugees. He then moved to Zurich, where the mainstream of Socialist and Anarchist discussion could be found. The message his political mentors put forth was that the "bourgeois world" was incorrigibly corrupt and must be destroyed — and Mussolini publicly agreed. As soon as the authorities learned of his "dangerous political views," they expelled him from the country.

Mussolini moved to Trento, which then belonged to Austria. In February 1909 he became secretary of the Chamber of Labor and editor of *Il Popolo*, the organ of the Italian Socialists who proposed the integration of the Trentino into the kingdom of Italy. But, within a few months, Mussolini was expelled from Trento by the Austrian authorities.

Mussolini now embarked on a career as agitator in the Socialist cause, working as a publicist and organizer. His reputation grew and, in 1910, he was made secretary of the Socialist Association in his native province of Forlì, where he founded a newspaper called *La Lotta di Classe* (The Class Struggle). He held the secretaryship until he moved into national politics at the Socialist Congress of 1912.

Nearly thirty years old, Mussolini began to exhibit traits which would soon become familiar to the world. Above all, he was possessed of the need for action — action without forethought. His career as a troublemaker had come into full bloom.

Giolitti undertook his colonial adventure, the Lybian War, in September 1911. Italy had an unemployed population in the south, which it needed to send off to foreign lands. Mussolini himself opposed the war, and he and other Socialist leaders spoke out against it. Mussolini was one of the most violent anti-war speakers and, as a proponent of open resistance to the government, was often arrested. He engaged in numerous violent acts against the government, for which he was convicted and sentenced to five years in prison; but, on appeal, the sentence was reduced to five months.

After Mussolini's release from prison, the Socialists hailed him as a hero and martyr. At the Congress of Reggio Emilia in 1912, he was made editor of the Party newspaper, *Avanti*.

The years 1913 and 1914 saw great civil strife in Italy. Naturally, Mussolini used *Avanti* to support the cause of revolution. There were demonstrations and rabble-rouser speeches. In the south, government troops fired upon demonstrators. The unrest spread to the north, and it was expected that at any moment a Republic might be proclaimed at Rome.

At this point in his career, Mussolini's political philosophy encompassed the following: an uncompromising hatred of bourgeois values; the will to subvert such values, even through violence; a broad, vague sympathy for the workers and peasants of the nation; and the conviction that the shape of history is determined by energetic minorities rather than by lethargic majorities.

When World War I broke out, Mussolini's basic sympathy was with the Allies. The Socialist Congress of September 1914 declared strongly for neutrality at any cost, but Mussolini was opposed to neutrality and asked the Executive Committee of the Socialist Party to reverse its stance. The Committee refused and Mussolini, a minority of one, resigned from the party. The Committee retaliated by firing him as editor of *Avanti*.

Mussolini's break with the Socialist Party marks the beginning of Fascism in Italy. *Fasci di Azione Revoluzionaria* — Bands (sheaves) of Revolutionary Action — were formed and, under his leadership, began campaigning for intervention. There were

113

pro-war demonstrations all over the country, and on May 24 war was declared. Mussolini greeted the announcement with bitter words against the parliamentarians, whom he described as parasites.

Mussolini joined the army, but only after being conscripted. In February 1916 he was wounded and remained in the hospital until August 1917. He returned to his newspaper, *Popolo d'Italia*, not only as a simple political leader but now as a war hero as well.

Italy's situation was desperate. The army, poorly equipped and poorly trained, suffered severe losses; on the home front, defeat gripped the nation. There was a strong move to get out of the war, especially after the debacle at Caporetto.

The men who had fought for a just cause felt that their blood had been spilled in vain. Adding to the humiliation and sense of defeat, the Socialists conducted a bitter campaign of derision against those who had fought, designating them as dupes and fools.

Matters were made worse by the incompetence of the government, which had made no provisions for speedy demobilization, thereby giving substance to the Socialist claim that the Italian soldier had been used as a tool to further capitalist oppression. The swollen industries of war suddenly slumped, and unemployment rose until some four hundred thousand workers — out of almost four million — were without income.

In March 1919 Mussolini brought together a group of friends and associates and revived his *Fasci* as a political party. The *Fasci* now traveled around the country making revolutionary speeches and attacking the Socialists. The fledgling party soon began to grow; the people, particularly the workers, seemed ready for Fascism. Young people, disillusioned by disorder at home and reverses abroad, began to look to Fascism for salvation. Mussolini publicly claimed to be the champion of the peasant and the worker, meanwhile bands of black-shirted Fascist thugs, known as *Squadre* or *Camicie Nere* (Black Shirts), terrorized Socialist agitators and organizers.

In 1921, when the Giolitti government gave up hope of winning the support of the Socialists, it gave active support to Mussolini who, with his vigilante Black Shirts, was regarded as Italy's champion of law and order. Fascism's opposition to Socialist-inspired unrest won approval from the government, which now not only protected the Black Shirts from arrest for arson, assault, and even murder, but also provided them with arms and money. Meanwhile, the Black Shirts aggressively went after the Socialists, who suffered the destruction of their centers by the hundreds, and the murder of scores of their members.

The March on Rome, Via Sleeping Car

As a result of the continuing violence in Piedmont, Lombardy, Tuscany, and the Marches, by the middle of 1922 the power of the Socialist Party had been effectively broken and Fascism spread everywhere in the ascendancy. The continuing economic and social crisis brought down the Bonomi government in February 1922. Bonomi was replaced by Luigi Facta, whose premiership proved to be a deathblow to Italy's already moribund parliamentary system. The nation continued moving toward virtual anarchy.

Nothing could have pleased Mussolini more than the public's complete disenchantment with the parliamentary system. Judging correctly that his moment had come, he began a series of public addresses in which he declared that peace could be restored by the abolition of the democratic framework of the past and the installation of a strong government: a Fascist regime.

"Our program is simple," he said, "we wish to govern Italy . . . but what is needed is men of strength and will power." Everywhere Mussolini spoke, cries were heard of "To Rome! To Rome!" Finally, on October 16, 1922, at a meeting in Milan, plans for a coup were laid. On October 21 a great convention of Fascists was held at Naples, where Mussolini announced: "The hour has struck. Either they give us the government, or we shall take it by falling on Rome."

King Victor Emmanuel was shrewd enough to grasp the situation and requested that Mussolini come to Rome. On that night of October 29, 1922, Mussolini boarded a sleeping car of the Milan-Rome express and arrived in Rome the following morning. This was how the March on Rome was brought about — in a sleeping car to Rome.

Il Duce: 1922–1939

Once in the saddle, Mussolini began to polish his image as a moderate statesman. He informed the Deputies that he wished to govern through Parliament, but at the same time warned the Chamber that it was "liable to dissolution in two days or two years." He demanded full power from Parliament, which readily gave it to him.

Mussolini did much to please the general public. Socialist-inspired strikes were a thing of the past. He also simplified the tax system in such a way that the wealthy would bear a larger share of the burden.

In the foreign arena, Mussolini scored triumphs. In January 1924 he negotiated an agreement with the government of Yugoslavia, whereby the status of Fiume as a Free State was abolished, and Italy received the controversial port, as well as the Delta and Port Barros. For this achievement, Mussolini received the acclamation of all Italy and the country's highest honor, The Collar of the Annunziata.

By July 1924 Mussolini had induced Parliament to pass a law giving him the power to suppress newspapers for publishing false news or news intended to disturb public order, evoke class hatred, or attack the king, pope, religion, or state. The suppression of freedom of the press was merely the beginning.

The years from 1925 to 1929 marked Mussolini's transformation from the leader of a political party to a dictator. The monarchy was retained but Mussolini was now head of state, *Capo di Stato*, with absolute power and no longer responsible to Parliament but to the Crown alone. Moreover, he could now rule by decree.

The Fascists took over the entire structure of the administrative and civil services. They held complete control over the state as well as the media. Newspaper editors who did not comply with the Fascists' orders would receive a visit from Mussolini's OVRA, the inevitable secret police. Continued resistance to Fascist dictates would result in banishment to one of Italy's tiny islands.

Italy's educational system was reorganized, with the aim of producing a generation schooled in the values of Fascism, rather than in the customary humanistic studies.

To his credit, however, Mussolini engaged in an enterprise that was to be the most brilliant success of his career: the reconciliation between Italy and the Vatican. Since 1870, the pope had been the self-proclaimed "prisoner of the Vatican," claiming that he had been deprived of what was rightfully his. The matter had not been resolved until the time of Mussolini.

Working steadily at reconciliation, negotiations were begun as early as 1926. On February 11, 1929, the Lateran treaty was signed. While the Holy See recognized the existence of the kingdom of Italy, Italy recognized the Holy See as a sovereign power.

Convinced that no European power would dare attempt more than hurl angry words at Italy, Mussolini ordered Marshal Badoglio, the Italian commander in East Africa, to launch a major offensive against the forces of Haile Selassie, which he did on January 12, 1936. On May 5, after a campaign of four months, Addis Ababa, the Emperor's capital city, fell. A few days later, Mussolini announced the annexation of Abyssinia and the King of Italy's assumption of the title, Emperor of Abyssinia. The King rewarded Mussolini with Italy's highest military decoration, the grand Cross of the Order of Savoy. Reflecting on the fact that Hitler was the only European potentate who did not disapprove of his African venture, Mussolini mused that "the Axis was born in 1936."

The plunge into the fatal Axis continued at a fast pace. Next came Mussolini's support of Spain's military revolt, led by General Franco in July 1936, only two months after the African victory. By the middle of 1936, Italian aid to Franco had increased to an estimated seventy thousand Italian troops fighting against the Republicans.

Then came the surrender of the Sudetenland and, on March 15, the German troops' march into Czechoslovakia. That night, Hitler proudly announced to the world: "Czechoslovakia has ceased to exist."

The Vatican Swiss Guards.

1939 to 1945: The End

Was it in emulation of Hitler that on April 7, 1938, Mussolini had his troops land in Albania? On the following day, April 8, the capital city of Tirana fell to the invading forces, while King Zog and his family fled to Greece. On April 16 King Victor Emmanuel added to his Crown Albania, which now became an Italian province.

Then followed all of the other German moves that led to Apocalypse: the non-aggression pact with the Soviet Union; the march on Poland on September 1, 1939; and the British and French declaration of war on Germany on September 3. As in 1914, Italy remained neutral.

In the spring of 1940 came the German invasion of Denmark, Norway, and Belgium. Even though he knew that intervention would plunge Italy into disaster, Mussolini found he could not help himself. On May 30 he announced to Hitler his intention to enter the war against the Allies, which he did on June 11.

Italy's plunge into disaster was quick: first, Germany invaded Russia, and Mussolini volunteered to send four Italian divisions in offensive support; then, the Japanese attacked Pearl Harbor on December 7; and, on December 11, Italy declared war on the United States, in company with Germany.

On October 23 General Montgomery defeated the Italian and German troops at El Alamein. Two weeks later, the entire Axis front collapsed. On November 7 the Allies landed in Morocco and Algeria. By May 13 of the following year, the Italian and German forces in Africa had surrendered to the Allies.

There was now open talk of the necessity of ridding Italy of the Fascists and discarding the fatal German alliance. News of the African disaster on May 13 gave the forces in Italy the courage to pull down the Fascist regime and Mussolini with it. *Il Duce* was now catapulted toward the end.

On July 9, 1943, Sicily fell to the Allies. The King knew that the time to act had come. He informed Mussolini that, in view of the fact that he no longer commanded the loyalty and confidence of the country, he must ask him to resign. When Mussolini attempted to argue, the King replied that "the solution could not have been otherwise" — he had already appointed Marshal Badoglio to form a new government. Accompanying the fallen Duce to the door, the King shook his hand, as Mussolini recorded, "with great warmth." Then, emerging from the royal villa, Mussolini was met by two police officers who escorted him, now a prisoner, to the *Caribinieri* barracks in Trastevere.

Badoglio made secret overtures of peace to the Allies and signed an armistice early in September. But the German troops held all of Italy north of Naples in their grip, and German paratroopers daringly rescued Mussolini from confinement, setting him up as the head of a Republican-Fascist government at Salò, in northern Italy.

In October 1944 Italy formally declared war on Germany, and the Allies, aided by Italian partisans, gradually pushed the Germans back up the peninsula. The following April, a band of partisans captured Mussolini and his mistress near Lake Como and summarily executed them. Their bodies were later strung up by the heels outside a gas station in Milan.

With Germany's surrender in May 1945, the war in Europe was over. Italy was free to adopt a democratic form of government as it moved toward the end of the century.

RECONSTRUCTION AND ITALY TODAY: 1945–2000

All in all, Italy emerged from the defeat of the Second World War more favorably than it had from the victory of the First World War. In the settlement of 1947, Italy lost possession of Africa and the Dodecanese islands, as well as Fiume and Istria. However, Italy was allowed to keep Trieste, the South Tyrol, and the Val d'Aosta. Moreover, while Britain and the United States forwent reparations, the latter supplied generous amounts of aid to help Italy through the postwar period. This was much-needed aid, for the war had left the peninsula physically devastated and its economy torn by inflation and mass unemployment.

The Italian Republic

Alcide De Gasperi, the ablest Italian statesman since Giolitti and leader of the Christian Democrats (DC), became premier in December 1945. Italy's future political direction was to a large extent decided on June 2, 1946, when the election took place for the constituent assembly. A new constitution was drawn up, and women had the right to vote for the first time.

In a referendum on the same day, Italians voted on whether the country would remain a monarchy or become a republic. The vote was in favor of the republic, and Umberto II, who only one month earlier had acceded to the throne on the abdication of his father, Vittorio Emanuele II, went into exile. Italy's first postwar election, held in April 1948, gave a huge majority to Premier De Gasperi's Christian Democrats. De Gasperi remained in office until his death in 1954.

The constitution was debated over for nearly two years. The final outcome was a constitution resembling that of the old Liberal state, minus the king. The nominal head of state was to be the president of the republic, elected by Parliament for a period of seven years; but the real power lay with the Council of Ministers and the legislature, which consisted of a Chamber of Deputies and the Senate, both elected by proportional representation. Judges were independent, controlled by a Supreme Council of the Judiciary. There was a Constitutional Court, and citizens had the right to challenge laws by means of popular referenda. Regional governments were set up, and the bureaucracy was decentralized. The 1929 Lateran Agreements with the Vatican, granting the clergy special privileges and outlawing divorce, were to be incorporated into the constitution.

1948–1960

The constitution went into effect on January 1, 1948. The first president of the new Italian Republic was Luigi Einaudi, an economist and former governor of the Bank of Italy, but not a member of the Christian Democrats. The first parliamentary elections were held on April 18, and the Christian Democrats won with a clear majority.

De Gasperi and the Christian Democrats

De Gasperi held power without interruption from 1948 to 1953. His governments, based on a number of coalitions, laid the essential foundations of postwar Italy. Apart from being a statesman, he was an agile and resourceful politician. In espousing the politics of accommodation, he set an example to his successors. A devout Catholic, he was wise enough not to pander to the wishes of the Church. Thus, in his eight cabinets he included non-Catholics as well as Liberals, Republicans, and Social Democrats. De Gasperi, an able statesman, provided Italy with the political stability necessary for reconstruction.

The most pressing challenge for the new republic was economic reconstruction. The country had been devastated by Fascism and the war. Many Italians lived in poverty in overcrowded rural houses and foul slums in and around the big cities; many families were even forced for a period to take shelter in caves.

But there was help. The Marshall Plan gave Italy large amounts of aid, and this along with additional aid from the United States helped develop efficient steel and cement industries. Additionally, Enrico Mattei's discovery of natural gas in the Po Valley was of great importance to a country with few natural resources.

Apart from overseeing the beginning of the reconstruction of the economy, De Gasperi was responsible for steering Italy into the position it currently holds within the international community: a firm member of the Western Alliance and a staunch supporter of European integration.

The Christian Democrat vote dropped to around forty percent in the 1953 elections, and this ended De Gasperi's political career. He died the following year, leaving a void in Italian politics. An array of governments and prime ministers came and went between 1953 and 1960 — Pella, Fanfani, Scelba, Segni, Zola, and Tambroni — all contributing to the party's retention of power.

The Other Parties

The Communist Party (PCI) under Togliatti remained the most important of the Left groups. It failed to provide a genuine alternative government, or even effective parliamentary opposition. Perhaps its greatest successes were in local government, where it came to be regarded as the party of good and incorruptible rule — Bologna, Florence, Milan, Turin, and Genoa all came under its control.

The Socialists never succeeded in wresting the leadership of the anti-DC movement from the Communists. On the extreme Right, the standard bearers of neo-Fascism, the MSI, polled around five to six percent of the vote.

The Economy Surges in the 1960s

While the economic recovery of the late 1940s and 1950s had been impressive, it hardly compared to what followed in the 1960s. The latter period is often referred to as the Italian "economic miracle." The country's Gross National Product more than doubled and industrial production more than tripled between 1951 and 1963. It was an export-led boom spearheaded by the leaders of Italian industry, FIAT, Montecatini-Edison, and Olivetti. But it was also the Italian spirit of improvisation and enterprise that came to the fore, as new firms mushroomed and whole industries began to dominate world markets.

Aldo Moro

The dominant political figure of the 1960s responsible for the DC's opening to the Left was Aldo Moro, who was prime minister from December 1963 to June 1968. He and his administration dealt with the slowdown of the "economic miracle" and the fundamental social changes affecting Italy. The cost of labor had risen, and there was a massive flight of capital from Italy to places such as Switzerland.

The economic downturn, as well as a series of scandals in the DC ranks, undermined Italy's credibility. By the late 1960s key functions in the cities, such as housing, education, transport, welfare, and medical services, had virtually broken down. The country was again poised to enter a period of turbulence.

The 1970s: Cultural Revolution and Terrorism

Italy's turbulence in the 1970s can be traced back to November 1967, when shipyard workers went on strike in Genoa and Trieste. This paved the way for an outbreak of unofficial strikes and protests, as the workers' anger mounted in a way that the official unions could not handle.

At the same time, the students were in ferment. The university system practically ceased to function. The student population had increased by fifty percent, while educational standards had declined sharply; by the mid-1970s, industry was employing only half as many graduates as it had in 1969. Thus, a large band of disaffected, educated young people evolved, their anger finding an outlet in the active and radical *movimento studentesco*, or student movement.

The autumn of 1969 was Italy's "hot autumn," as the country endured waves of strikes and demonstrations which continued into the early 1970s. Yet these disturbances brought unity to the trade union movement, which in turn achieved significant victories for the workers: a rapid wage increase and, in 1972, an entitlement to one hundred and fifty annual hours of paid education. The right not to be dismissed on economic grounds was established in 1975, guaranteeing at least eighty percent of full pay to laid-off workers.

In the social sphere, divorce became legal in 1970 to the chagrin of the Vatican. Controlled abortion was introduced in 1978 in response to the demands of the growing women's movement.

On the flip side, increased production costs resulting from large pay increases priced many Italian goods out of the market. Profits slumped, bankruptcies increased, and investments plunged. The economy and the basic fabric of society were in tatters. Yet despite all this, the national income still managed to increase by an average of about three percent during the 1970s.

Then, terrorism raised its ugly head. A bomb, exploding at the Piazza Fontana in Milan in 1969, killed sixteen people; Neo-Fascist terrorists derailed the Rome-Munich express in 1974, killing twelve; and a bomb placed in the Bologna railway station in 1980 killed eighty-four innocent bystanders. Meanwhile, the number of extreme Left-wing groups multiplied, financing themselves through kidnappings and bank robberies or else receiving money from rich sympathizers. At its height, red terrorism claimed forty victims a year in about two thousand incidents.

Anyone in authority was fair game for the terrorists, with policemen and DC politicians the favorite targets. The most outrageous "action" of the Red Brigades was the kidnapping and murder of Aldo Moro in 1978. In the early 1980s the Red Brigades and the other groups were crushed by the Carabinieri, under General della Chiesa. In 1992 della Chiesa, Prefect of Palermo, was killed by the Mafia.

At the Threshold of the Twenty-First Century

In general, Italy has continued on the path to becoming a thoroughly modern, open society, with a respected place within the European community. The state restored its authority over the country, thanks to the popular presidency of Sandro Pertini between 1978 and 1985. The country was shaken, however, by continual scandals involving the leading officials of the Christian Democrats.

Most significant has been the emergence of the Northern Leagues — such as the Lombard League, led by Umberto Bossi — which are Right-wing, anti-Mafia, anti-Rome, anti-immigrant, anti-tax, anti-South separatist parties. The Northern Leagues gained 8.5 percent of the popular vote in the 1992 elections.

The DC's vote fell sharply in 1983, recovered a little in 1987, only to fall back to a historical low of 29.7 percent in 1992. It managed to recapture the position of prime minister in the late eighties and early nineties; but the current prime minister, Massimo d'Alema, is a member of the *Partito Democratico di Sinistra*

(The Democratic Party of the Left) — the name adopted by the vast majority of the Communist Party in 1991 after it underwent a fundamental ideological crisis and division.

The Cultural Scene

During the twentieth century, Italy produced some of the world's greatest artists, musicians, poets, novelists, and cinematographers, and garnered a total of six Nobel Prizes in Literature.

Giosuè Carducci (1835–1907).

In poetry, the century opened with the work of Giosuè Carducci (1835–1907). Born in Tuscany, he was professor of literature at the University of Bologna from 1860 to 1904. In 1906 he was awarded the Nobel Prize in Literature, becoming the first Italian to receive that honor. His poetry is classic in form, with a deep and wide range of emotion. His chief works include *Rime* (Rhymes), *Inno a Satana* (Hymn to Satan), and *Rime Nuove* (New Rhymes).

The Nobel Prize in Literature was awarded to two other distinguished Italian poets during the century. One of the outstanding Italian poets since Dante and Petrarch was Salvatore Quasimodo (1901–1968). Had he not written poetry, he would be remembered as the gifted translator of the Greek and Latin classics, including *Greek Lyrics, Catullus, Selections from the Odyssey, Euripides' Hecuba* and *Heracles, Ovid's Metamorphoses, Sophocles' Oedipus King* and *Elektra*. Brilliant are his poetic translations of Shakespeare's *Romeo and Juliet, Richard III, Othello, Macbeth,* and *The Tempest*, as well as his translation of Molière's *Tartuffe*.

Sixteen years later, in 1975, the Nobel Prize in Literature was bestowed upon another Italian poet, Eugenio Montale (1896–1981). Focusing on the human condition, Montale's poetry tends to be abstract and intellectual, belonging to the "hermetic" school of poetry. It is also sad and pessimistic, a reflection of Montale's own nature. In fact, upon learning that he had been awarded the Nobel Prize in Literature, he stated: "I am overwhelmed . . . I am happy. This makes my life, which has always been unhappy, less unhappy." In fifty years, Montale published only five books of poetry: *The Occasion, The Storm and Other Things, Satura, Diary of '71 and of '72,* and *Cuttlefish Shells*.

The poet who created and most represented Italian hermetic poetry was Giuseppe Ungaretti (1888–1970). His particular hermetic "technique of obscuration" is an outcropping of two French symbolists, Guillaume Apollinaire and Stéphane Mallarmé, who were his acquaintances during his years in Paris. Ungaretti's principal works are *Joy, Grief, The Feeling of Time,* and *Life of a Man*. He was the recipient of numerous literary prizes.

Salvatore Quasimodo (1901–1968).

Eugenio Montale (1896–1981).

The theater was dominated by Luigi Pirandello (1867–1936), Italy's 1934 Nobel Laureate in Literature. Pirandello ranked among the greatest Italian dramatists of the twentieth century, and his plays were translated into all western European languages; some were made into movies, and a number were hits on Broadway, as well as in Paris, Berlin, and Buenos Aires. Pirandello wrote a total of fifty-six plays — twelve in his Sicilian dialect, which he considered a worthy literary medium, and forty-four in Italian.

Pirandello also wrote novels and short stories, the latter distinguishing him as one of the greatest writers of all time. But it was the theater that heaped him with praise and honors around the world. Urged by his friends to write for the theater, he found that he could turn out plays with ease and efficiency — dramas that penetrated and depicted the human character, psychology, and motivation. *The License, The Vise, Sicilian Limes, Six Characters in Search of an Author,* and *Henry IV* were among his masterpieces. Pirandello is noted for having explored two themes: the world of fantasy, at times bordering on insanity as it invades and dominates life; and relativity, as it affects character in human beings.

Italy can take pride in two other inventive playwrights of the twentieth century: Dario Fo, the 1997 Nobel Laureate in Literature, and France Rame. Italy has also been a world leader in cinematography with such acclaimed directors as de Sica, Visconti, Rossellini, Antonioni, Fellini, Pasolini, Rosi, Zeffirelli, and Bertolucci, and with such stars as Anna Magnani, Sophia Loren, Gina Lollobrigida, and Marcello Mastroianni.

In fiction, the century opened with Giovanni Verga (1840–1922). He was born in Catania, Sicily, and as a young man lived

Luigi Pirandello (1867–1936).

in Florence and Milan, where he wrote several drawing-room novels in the French realist style.

When Verga returned to Sicily, he began writing about the humble people of his land; these masterpieces, although written in Italian, reflected the simplicity of his native Sicilian. One of the short stories in his *Novelle rusticane*, the *Cavalleria rusticana,* was turned into Pietro Mascagni's popular opera of that name (1890). *The House by the Medlar Tree* and *Mastro Don Gesualdo* are his other notable masterpieces. D.H. Lawrence, upon discovering Verga, could find only one word adequate to his primitive depth and power: Homeric.

Shortly after Verga, the works of one of the first Italian female novelists appeared on the literary landscape. Grazia Deledda (1875–1936), a Sardinian, had her first collection of short stories published when she was nineteen. Awarded the Nobel Prize in Literature in 1926, her novels are naturalistic, lyrical, and contain touches of violence and humor. Her work has been compared to that of George Sand and Chekhov. Her novels include *After the Divorce* (1902); *Elias Portolú* (1903); *Ashes* (1904); *Reeds in the Wind* (1913); *The Mother* (1920); and *Flight into Egypt* (1925).

One of the most important and prolific of the modern Italian novelists was Alberto Moravia (1907–1990). His first published novel, *The Time of Indifference*, in 1929, was an immediate success. The following year, Moravia became a journalist, but never ceased his creative writing.

Moravia's works focused on a single theme: the disintegration of middle-class mores as revealed through the prism of sex. Widely read in the United States, *The Indifferent, The Wheel of Fortune, The Garden Party, The Woman of Rome*, and *The Conformist* were among his most popular works. During his lifetime, Moravia received several literary awards.

Alberto Moravia (1907–1990).

Italy has had other first-rate novelists, including Vasco Pratolini, Cesare Pavese, Ignazio Silone, Elio Vittorini, Umberto Eco, and Leonardo Scascia. Yet the most significant novelist may well be Giuseppe Tomasi, Duke of Palma and Prince of Lampedusa (1896–1957).

The Tomasis belonged to the last of a fading Sicilian aristocracy, which dates back to the Norman eleventh century and which ended in 1860, when Garibaldi routed the Bourbons from Italy and lower Italy. It is this period in Sicilian history that Lampedusa depicts in his masterpiece, *Il Gattopardo* (The Leopard): the fading old aristocracy awkwardly finding a place in the new bourgeois society.

On Lampedusa's deathbed, the manuscript of *Il Gattopardo* was sent anonymously to Elena Craveri Croce, Benedetto Croce's daughter, in Rome, who soon forgot about it. Then it was sent to a publisher in Milan, who gave it to the Sicilian novelist, Elio Vittorini, to read. Before he died, Lampedusa received a letter from Vittorini, who was returning the manuscript which he had read but turned down because it was too "essayish."

Tomasi read and re-read the letter and said: "It was kind of him to take so much trouble. You can see that he read it carefully. What a pity." Prince Lampedusa died without ever having seen his novel published.

But there is a happy ending after all. The novelist, Giorgio Bassani, then editorial chief of the Feltrinelli publishing house, read the manuscript Elena Croce had sent to him after Lampedusa's death. Immediately, he rushed to Palermo. At the author's home, Bassani discovered another manuscript in the author's own handwriting, which contained important additions. This is the final version that Feltrinelli published.

There was also a glorious era of Italian music in the twentieth century. *Cavalleria rusticana* by Mascagni and the *Pagliacci* by Leoncavallo deserve mention. But above all, Giacomo Puccini (1858–1924) was master of the opera.

Puccini's first opera, *Le Villi,* performed in 1883, was followed by a stream of operas which are still loved today by audiences around the world — *Manon Lescaut, La Bohème, Tosca, The Girl of the Golden West, Il tabarro, La rondine, Suor Angelica, Madame Butterfly,* and his last opera, *Turandot.*

The Golden Age of Italian Opera closed the twentieth century with a curtain call for its great composers and singers: Caruso, Tito Schipa, Beniamino Gigli, Tito Ruffo, Galli Curci, Rosa Ponselle, and Ezio Pinza.

Giacomo Puccini (1858–1924).

AFTERWORD

Italy's chaotic history can be summarized in the following statement appearing earlier in this study: "It was a period during which Italy was defenseless and helpless, under the control of powerful foreign nations. That it had created modern civilization for Europe availed it not at all."

From the Roman Empire's collapse until the arrival of Garibaldi in 1860, Italy's neighbors — Austria, Spain, and France — continually vied for pieces of the country and annexed it to their own. Most of the time, Spain owned half of the peninsula and the islands of Sicily and Sardinia, while the north fell under Austrian control. The middle part was at one time or another dominated or controlled by the papacy. Curiously, it was the papacy which, thinking of enhancing its own power, introduced the idea of a national political control.

These foreign masters cared little about the welfare of the people, and more about power and money. This was the tenor of the feudal system which had a strangle hold on the country and the people. Possibly, the greatest Italian hero was not Mazzini or Cavour, but Garibaldi, who with his handful of adventurous followers routed the foreign enemy and handed the country over to a native monarchy to form a greater Italy. His invasion in 1860 initiated the nascent republic's quest for national identity and freedom. Italy acquired both in the twentieth century, except for a short interruption by Mussolini and his gangsters. But once Mussolini was removed, Italy was able to resume democratic statehood, bringing it into line with the other democracies of western Europe.

Once free, all else followed: literacy, education, economic development, and national identity. Italy's culture had pervaded, despite past invasions and subjugation by foreign masters. In the thirteenth and fourteenth centuries Dante and his colleagues forged a new language and created Italian poetry. With this early Renaissance, Italy began to assert its spirit, drawing from the Romans to build a new identity. From then on, no matter who seized control of the country, Italians thought of themselves as citizens of Italy — the descendants of glorious Rome. Now, in the twenty-first century, Italy is a proud republic, and the equal of its European neighbors.

It is a wonder that a country, which during a millennium and a half was bandied about by greedy neighbors and despoiled by voracious feudal lords, could produce one of the richest cultures — with some of the finest architecture, painting, sculpture, and literature — in the world. Italians can be justly proud of such accomplishments, and look to the twenty-first century with pride and optimism.

INDEX

Aldo Moro, 126, 128
Alexander VI, 35, 60, 62, 63, 65
Alfonso of Aragon, 32

Badoglio, 118, 121
Barbarians, 2, 3, 6
Bellini, 103
Boccaccio, 19, 23
Botticelli, 28

Carbonari, 78, 80
Carducci, 129
Caruso, 138
Cavour, 79–80, 88, 89, 90,
    92–99, 103, 139
Charlemagne, 8, 10
Charles VIII, 32, 60, 61, 62
Christian Democrats, 122, 123,
    124, 125, 126, 128
Cosimo de' Medici, 23–25, 26
Crispi, 88, 105

Dante, 17–20, 23, 80, 100,
    130, 140
De Gasperi, 122, 123–124
Deledda, 135

Eugenius IV, 34

Fo, 133
Frederick II, 14, 17

Garibaldi, 2, 79, 80, 83, 84–92,
    96, 98, 99, 103, 137, 139
Giolitti, 106–107, 112, 115, 122
Giotto, 19

Jesuits, 70
Julius II, 35, 40, 45, 63
Justinian I, 6

Lampedusa, 137
Leonardo da Vinci, 44, 45
Leoncavallo, 138
Leopardi, 77, 100, 103
Lombard League, 14, 128
Lombards, 6–7, 8, 11, 95, 96
Lorenzo the Magnificent, 25–30,
    44, 52, 60
Louis XII, 61–63
Luigi Einaudi, 123

Manzoni, 100–101, 103
Maria Theresa, 69, 70, 71
Martin V, 33, 34
Mascagni, 135, 138
Mazzini, 79, 80–84, 86, 92, 99,
    103, 139
Metternich, 75, 76
Michelangelo, 26, 35, 44, 45, 52
Montale, 130
Moravia, 135
Mussolini, 109–121, 139

Napoleon, 2, 72–75, 76, 92, 95, 97
Nicholas V, 34, 35, 43

Odoacer, 6
Ostrogoths, 2, 6
Otto the Great, 10

Petrarch, 19, 44, 130
Philip II, 65–66
Pippin, 8
Pirandello, 133
Pope Gregory I, 8
Puccini, 138

Quasimodo, 130

Rame, 133
Raphael, 35, 44, 45

Renaissance, 21–60
Risorgimento, 75–103
Robert of Anjou, 30
Romulus, 3, 6
Rossini, 103

Saracens, 2, 10–11, 12
Savonarola, 61
Sforza, Francesco, 43

Togliatti, 125
Treaty of Aix-la-Chapelle, 69

Verdi, 13, 100, 101–103
Verga, 133, 135
Victor Emmanuel I, 74, 76
Visconti, Gian Galeazzo, 42

Other Illustrated Histories from Hippocrene Books. . .

The Celtic World: An Illustrated History 700 B.C. to the Present

Patrick Lavin

From the valleys of Bronze Age Urnfielders to the works of 20TH century Irish-American literary greats Mary Higgins Clark and Seamus Heaney, Patrick Lavin leads the reader on an entertaining and informative journey through 182 captivating pages of Celtic history, culture, and tradition, including 50 illustrations and maps.

191 pages • 5 x 7 • 50 b/w illus./maps • $14.95hc • 0-7818-0731-X • W • (582)

England: An Illustrated History

Henry Weisser

English history is a rich and complex subject that has had a major influence on the development of the language, laws, institutions, practices, and ideas of the United States and many other countries throughout the world. Just how did all of this originate over the centuries in this pleasant, green kingdom? This concise, illustrated volume traces the story from England's most distant past to the present day, highlighting important political and social developments as well as cultural achievements.

166 pages • 5 x 7 • 50 b/w illus./maps • $11.95hc • 0-7818-0751-4 • W • (446)

Ireland: An Illustrated History

Henry Weisser

Erin go bragh! While it is easy to appreciate the natural beauty of Ireland, the Emerald Isle's history is also a rich and complex subject of study. Spanning prehistoric and Celtic Ireland to modern times, this concise, illustrated volume examines the people, religion, social changes, and politics that have evolved into the tradition of modern Ireland.

166 pages • 5 x 7 • 50 b/w illus./maps • $11.95hc • 0-7818-0693-3 • W • (782)

Israel: An Illustrated History

David C. Gross

Despite its physical size, Israel from earliest times to the present has always been a major player on the world stage. This concise, illustrated volume offers the reader an informative, panoramic view of this remarkable land, from biblical days to the 21ST century. With topics exploring art, literature, sculpture, music, science, politics, religion and more, here is a wonderful gift book for travelers, students, or anyone seeking to expand their knowledge of Israeli history, culture, and heritage.

148 pages • 5 x 7 • 50 b/w illus./maps • $11.95hc • 0-7818-0756-5 • W • (24)

Mexico: An Illustrated History

Michael Burke

This handy historical guide traces Mexico from the peasant days of the Olmecs to the late 20TH century. With over 150 pages and 50 illustrations, the reader discovers how events of Mexico's past have left an indelible mark on the politics, economy, culture, spirit, and growth of this country and its people.

183 pages • 5 x 7 • 50 b/w illus. • $11.95hc • 0-7818-0690-9 • W • (585)

Poland in World War II: An Illustrated Military History

Andrew Hempel

This illustrated history is a concise presentation of the Polish military war effort in World War II, intermingled with factual human interest stories and 50 black-and-white photos and illustrations.

117 pages • 5 x 7 • 50 b/w illus. • $11.95hc • 0-7818-0758-1 • W • (541)

Russia: An Illustrated History

Joel Carmichael

Encompassing one-sixth of the earth's land surface—the equivalent of the whole North American continent—Russia is the largest country in the world. Renowned historian Joel Carmichael presents Russia's rich and expansive past—upheaval, reform, social change, growth—in an easily accessible and concentrated volume. From the Tatar's reign to modern-day Russia, the book spans seven centuries of cultural, social and political events.

252 pages • 5 x 7 • 50 b/w illus. • $14.95hc • 0-7818-0689-5 • W • (781)

Prices subject to change without notice. **To purchase Hippocrene Books** contact your local bookstore, call (718) 454-2366, or write to: HIPPOCRENE BOOKS, 171 Madison Avenue, New York, NY 10016. Please enclose check or money order, adding $5.00 shipping (UPS) for the first book and $.50 for each additional book.

3 1221 07473 3010